Real Feedback for *Think It* from Real People

Here's what early readers and my clients have to say about what you'll learn in *Think It.* Follow my journey, let me know your thoughts on Substack @sarahcentrella or on Instagram @sarahcentrella, and I'll respond! I'd love to hear your wins using these tools. Be sure to tag me and use the hashtag #ThinkIt and join my free #ThinkItChallenge at the end of this book to kick off your own mental fitness journey.

"Sarah slices right through the ambiguity of most mindset advice and focuses on the practical steps that anyone can take to fundamentally change what's not working in their lives. As a self-made woman who has achieved everything she set out to manifest and more, Sarah is precise, direct, and is as real as they come!"

—**Nancy Bruce** | Dating Coach |
Host of *Finding Love* podcast

"I've been fortunate to be part of Sarah's life since 2010, and I've seen her apply the principles and methods she writes about to elevate her own life and the lives of her children. I've witnessed her words and mindset become her real life and give life to those around her. Her mindset created her success, and now she's sharing those tools with the world."

—**Kenjon Barner** | Three-Time Super Bowl
Champion | Big Ten Network Contributor

"*Think It* is more than a mindset book, it's the playbook for anyone who wants to put in the reps to win on or off the field."

—**A'Lique Terry** | Offensive Line Coach at the University of Oregon

"*Think It* is the mindset manual I wish I had during my darkest days—Sarah gives you the tools to rise stronger, with grit and grace."

—**Amberly Lago** | Bestselling Author of *Joy Through the Journey* | TEDx Speaker

"Being able to use Sarah's Mental Tennis to knock negative thoughts out of my head when I'd mess up in a game or a practice, for the first time ever, was something that allowed me to thrive under pressure. If people try this tool, I know it will work for them too."

—**Josh Conerly Jr.** | Washington Commanders 2025 First Round Draft Pick

"Sarah is an exceptional friend, coach, and writer. Her mindset tools are simple, actionable and her passion for helping people train their mindset shines through in this book."

—**Korey McCray** | Florida Gators Men's Basketball Associate Head Coach | 2025 NCAA National Champion

"I can't put this book down!"

—**@audralynnbruemmer** (Substack)

"This is SO good, Sarah!! You know I love your work, and have read all your books, but I can tell this one is something special. Learning these tools from you over the past few years has changed my life in ways I never expected. You've helped change my mindset, brought clarity and helped me create the life I always dreamed of. And this is only the beginning!"

—**Amanda Cahill** | Client | Branch Communications Executive Vice President of Sales and Development | Author of *Redefining You* | @amandacahill__ (Instagram)

"Wow! I can't wait for this to be released. I'm a mental health therapist and I have several clients who would greatly benefit from this book. I love that it's written in a way anyone can understand and apply what you are saying, such good stuff!"

—**April Fjeld** | MA, MEd, LCMHCA | @aprilf123 (Substack)

"Working with Sarah changed my life! When I met her a few years ago I was really unhappy in my life and career. She helped me change my mindset, set my vision, and get clear about what I wanted. Using her tools I was able to leave a job I disliked, and cofound a very successful law firm, and today I can honestly say I'm happier in all areas of my life than I've ever been! These tools work!"

—**Bonnie Page** | Client | Attorney and Cofounder of Macro Law Group

"*Think It* is like your first coffee of the day, but for your mind!"

—**@shellyroberts** (Substack)

"I love your unique style and approach to mindset—you're so relatable. Using the I AM Statements has helped me go from disliking my body my whole life, to loving it!"

—**LaParis McGowan** @laparisunedeesse (Substack)

"I love how matter-of-fact you present these normally intense concepts—and thank you for the incredibly real tone you use! So relatable. You make it so easy to understand and apply. See it. Stop it. Replace it. Thank you!!"

—**@christopherseippvercnocke** (Instagram)

"Wow! I've been rewiring my brain for just over a month and already I'm seeing the changes. One of the big impacts is that I have become less anxious and stressed."

—**@footstepconversations** (Substack)

"As someone who's worked with Sarah, first as a coaching client, then training with her to become a life coach certified in her methods, I can honestly say—it's been life changing. Her tools are not wishful thinking or positive fluff. They are practical, powerful, and work when you apply them. Since starting this work I've gained clarity, reprogrammed limiting beliefs, and gained a level of confidence I've never had. I love these tools and methods so much. Here's the thing, this process works, I'm living proof!"

—**Deanna Brown** | Client | Certified Centrella Method™ Life Coach | @deannabrown_collective (Instagram)

"I love this book and the *Think It* tools so much. When I started working with Sarah I felt like I just 'was who I was,' and that my life couldn't be changed. But these tools have helped me create and manifest a life I could barely dream of, and it still blows my mind! Changing my mindset with the *Think It* tools (especially the Energy Bubble and I AM Statements) has changed every part of my life, from relationships to career and everything in between."

—**Stephanie Holmes** | Client

"*Think It* is an absolute must read if you want to transform your life and go from where you are to where you want to be."

—**Brad Carlson** @ronin0725 (Substack)

"Before reading this book and learning your techniques, I never realized how much self talk can hold a person back. Thank you for showing us how to change that."

—**Julie Slaikjer** @julieslaikjer (Substack)

"Sarah, you have an amazing gift! You offer valuable guidance to your clients and tools that work. I've seen the positive impact your coaching and techniques have had on my entire team and always look forward to our sessions!"

—**Brandi Frye** | Client | Qorvo
Corporate VP of Marketing

"Sarah, you are so relatable and I know that so many people are going to have their lives changed through reading *Think It*, hearing your stories and then, of course, doing the work. I love Mental Tennis and have been using it for years since taking one of your group coaching programs, it is a game changer!"

—**Merridy Smits** @merridysmits2 (Substack)

"*Think It* is more than just a personal growth book—it's a mental reset, a soul tune-up and a tool box for real transformation all in one. The tools Sarah shares here—Power Mottos, Mental Tennis, I AM Statements, and the Energy Bubble—weren't just helpful, they are a game changer! Each one helped me identify and change self-sabotaging behavior and limiting beliefs. But what's truly unique about this book is Sarah herself. Her raw relatable coaching style cut right to the heart and empowered me to [do] the work. Because of these tools I've radically shifted my mindset around success, abundance, ownership and what is possible for my life. And I've already gotten the wins to prove it!"

—**@cameron.seippvercnocke.re** (Instagram)

"*Think It* is a book like no other, the one I've been searching for to teach me how to change my mindset. Sarah's tools such as Power Mottos and the Energy Bubble are ones I use regularly to create my next level of success."

—**Lara Folks**

Also by Sarah Centrella

All the Things I Wish I Knew: How to Be a Fierce Chick Living Her Best Life

THINK IT

How to Train Your Thinking to Get Everything You Want

SARAH CENTRELLA

Post Hill Press

A POST HILL PRESS BOOK
ISBN: 979-8-89565-420-0
ISBN (eBook): 979-8-89565-421-7

Think It:
How to Train Your Thinking to Get Everything You Want

Cover design by Sarah Centrella

Post Hill Press
New York • Nashville
posthillpress.com

Published in the United States of America
1 2 3 4 5 6 7 8 9 10

For Jeremiah, I will forever try to make you proud.

Float easy little brother.

And for Kanen, Mira, and Izzy, my reason for everything.

Table of Contents

PART THREE: *THINK IT* IN ACTION:
HOW TO APPLY THE TOOLS IN REAL LIFE

Preface

Started from the Bottom

How One Thought Changed My Life

I'll never forget the first time I heard, "You can change your thoughts." It was from Louise Hay on *The Oprah Winfrey Show*. This must have been 2006 or '07, and I remember thinking, *What is she talking about? How is that even possible?*

I was so unaware at the time, with no interest in or exposure to personal development or the concept of self-help. It wasn't mainstream popular back then, the way it is today. There were no social media #thinkpositive or #MindsetIsEverything hashtags, no inspirational T-shirts. Honestly, I probably found that episode and conversation a bit over my head and boring, yet somehow the idea stuck. It nagged at me.

How could I change my thoughts? I wondered. *Why would I want to? Didn't my brain just think thoughts on its own?* The whole idea was baffling. It made no sense to me. *Maybe I'm just stupid,* I remember thinking. *Maybe big, esoteric ideas like trying to control your mind are for people a lot smarter than me.*

At the time, I was a thirty-four-year-old stay-at-home mom with infant twin daughters and a five-year-old son. I was married to my high school sweetheart and trying hard not to collapse under the pressure and exhaustion of three little kids. My husband had suddenly grown distant. I was forty pounds heavier than a few years before and hated how I looked. All day, every day, the voice in my head ripped me apart, telling me how fat and gross I was.

Financially, our life was imploding. We'd lost our house to foreclosure the previous year in the collapse of the housing bubble, our car had been repossessed, and we'd just filed for bankruptcy. The unpaid bills were piling up. It felt like life was swallowing us whole. The voice in my head constantly reminded me what a failure I was, insisted there was no hope, and predicted that things would only get worse.

And of course, they did.

In September 2008, I read a text message that blew up my entire life.

It was from my husband's mistress, and it ended our marriage in about ten minutes. He was in the shower, soap covering his face, when I turned the water off and told him to "get the fuck out."

He didn't protest, just got out of the shower, still covered in soap and dripping wet, reached for his clothes, and pulled them on while I watched from the hallway, stunned and shaking. I expected him to deny it, say it was all a mistake, that it didn't mean anything. But he didn't. He just walked past me and, without a word, went into each of our children's rooms and kissed them goodbye. I was shaking, with my arm pointing to the door, repeating the only words in my head: "Get the fuck out!" He walked to the front door, and before he stepped outside, he turned around to look at me and threw his wedding ring across the floor in my general direction.

I filed for divorce a week later.

If I thought life was rough before that shower, nothing prepared me for how bad it got after. We hadn't kept up on bills with his income, so how could I survive without it? What was I thinking? Now I had no income, no savings, no job. Even the bank accounts were in his name. How could I possibly take care of my babies? I felt so trapped and helpless.

And the voice in my head continued to scream at me the way it always did: *YOU'RE A FAILURE. YOU DESERVED THIS. This wouldn't have happened if you were better at money or a better wife. If you had lost the baby weight maybe you could get a job. See? Nothing good ever happens to you*—and on it droned.

Ever had a voice in your head sound like that? It's not helpful. It doesn't inspire you to greatness. It doesn't give you the energy to get out of bed or to pick up the pieces of your life, let alone the motivation to start over from scratch.

But something pivotal happened to me a few hours after my husband left. That night, when I lay on the floor crying my eyes out, thinking of all the ways I could never make this work—how I just couldn't do it alone—I heard a new internal voice. One I'd never heard before. It said…

What if you CAN?

That thought was like being tossed a lifeline on a capsized boat in the middle of an angry sea, and I clung to it ferociously. That tiny thought brought hope and possibility, a shred of positivity that sounded so utterly foreign yet so desperately needed. Instead of focusing on everything that was going wrong in my life, and all the worst-case scenarios, I started asking myself, *Well, what if I could? What would that look like?* That little positive "what if" began digging me out of my darkness and opening up ideas that helped me form a plan to reinvent my life.

In all the chaos and darkness that followed in the next several months, Louise Hay's words kept coming back to me: *You can change your thoughts, to change your future.*

I still didn't know if that was true or not. Honestly, I was skeptical. But the possibility it represented haunted me. I started paying more attention to what my head was telling me, and let's just say, it was depressing. I was so mean to myself—all day, every day. Like, what the fuck.

I'll never forget my first conscious experiment to change my thoughts. I had no idea what I was doing or if there was a "right way" to do it, but I figured whatever I tried was better than nothing. I was beginning to see the correlation between my continuous negative self-talk and my real life, and that realization stung. I didn't want to feel like shit anymore. Something had to change.

So, I went into the bathroom, looked myself in the eye, and said out loud: "I am beautiful. I look and feel incredible. I am sexy. I am loved. I am doing a good job. I am a good mom. I am good with money. I am successful."

I looked at my reflection and sobbed with each affirmation. With every single one, that nasty bitch voice in my head tried to scream and argue: *You are not beautiful,* it pointed out. *Look at you, you are a mess. No one will ever love you. You are failing at everything*

But I just repeated those damn affirmations louder each time. I showed up in that mirror every morning and every night and told myself all the things I wished I felt, wanted to believe, or dreamed of becoming. And slowly, I started to feel better. I started walking on my lunch breaks and using the apartment gym. When I felt tired and weak, I told myself, *I can do it. I am strong.* I started putting some effort into my appearance and imagining myself as a boss babe!

Then one day, I was finishing my makeup, about to go out with a friend, and I took one last look in the mirror. Without prompting, I automatically had the thought, for the very first time in my life: *Damn girl! You are beautiful. You look sexy tonight!* That magical transition from thought to reality had taken place somewhere along the way, and in that moment, I felt beautiful. It was no longer a lie.

I was like…*holy shit! Did I do that? Did it actually work?* I honestly never thought it would. I just wanted to feel better. I never imagined that it could genuinely change how I saw myself or how I felt. I was shocked.

And then I had an idea: *What if I could use this trick to change other things about myself and my life?* Maybe I could use it to change my financial situation (that seemed completely insane, by the way), or lose weight, or even use it to get a better job. Now I was getting excited!

That began my quest to find the hacks, the simple and easy ways to get my thoughts to start creating a new future. It's a journey that has completely changed my life, my children's lives, and the lives of thousands of clients and readers worldwide. And it's about to change yours too, if you are willing to do this work. Trust me, that's not cocky; it's facts. If you take the advice in this book seriously, do the journal work in each section as you read it, and practice the tools daily, it will change your life forever.

Think It is one of nine steps I teach every client, and it is by far the most important. It's the one that will have the most dramatic and near-instant impact on all aspects of your life.

So…are you ready to see what can happen in your life?

Let's do this!

Part One

Where It All Begins

How Your Thoughts Created the Life You Have and How to Use Them to Create the One You Really Want

Understanding Your Mind

Before we can change anything, we need to understand what's really going on in your head. We can't shift what we're not aware of, and most of us are walking around with a constant stream of thoughts that we've never questioned.

Part 1 lays the foundation for everything you'll learn in this book. It breaks down the science and psychology behind the *Think It* tools, why your thoughts are shaping your reality, how your subconscious beliefs are running the show behind the scenes, and what's actually happening when you spiral or self-sabotage.

You'll learn the key concepts of mental "offense" and "defense" and why mindset is about so much more than just thinking positively. This section gives you the awareness you need to finally take control of your thinking, and that's where real change begins.

It's important to know that these tools aren't just for people who want to completely change their life. They're just as powerful if you already love the life you've built. You can be proud of how far you've come and still want to grow, evolve, and create the next version of yourself and your success. That's exactly how I use them. Even though I love my life, I'm always focused on defining what's next and intentionally building my best-case future, while simultaneously being grateful for what I have.

So, if parts of this book about "changing your life" don't quite resonate, just think of it as *How do I expand? How can I use this tool to grow and step into my next chapter with intention?*

Chapter 1

It All Starts with a Thought

Why Thoughts Matter

Descartes said it best: "I think, therefore I am." In other words, my thoughts create me. But how does that actually happen? That was the first question I asked myself when I saw this quote on the cover of a journal in the checkout line at HomeGoods many years ago.

These are some of the questions I hear from clients every day. Maybe you can relate?

- Why do I keep sabotaging myself, even when I really want something?
- I feel stuck in a job or life that doesn't fulfill me. Is there anything I can do to change that?
- How do I figure out what's next?
- How do I stop the inner critic and constant self-doubt?

- I know I have a scarcity mindset. How do I change it?
- Why am I so overwhelmed, anxious, or exhausted all the time?
- I want to feel confident and successful, but I don't know how.
- How do I stop repeating patterns that keep holding me back?
- I want to build wealth and peace, but I'm stuck in survival mode.

What do all these questions and statements have in common? They all start with a thought.

What I'm about to teach you isn't rocket science. It's not "positive thinking" or toxic positivity. It's not New Age feel-good fluff or a cool slogan like "Mindset is Everything" on a yoga shirt. This is common sense. You're about to learn a logical process for training your thoughts to start getting what you want and stop getting what you don't. This is HOW you change your thinking—in the moment—so you can be the person you want to be, living the life you deserve. I call it "mental fitness," and it's about to change your entire world.

Just like every other muscle in your body, your mind needs training and regular workouts to stay on track and deliver peak performance. But most people, like how I was in 2008, have no idea how to manage the constant stream of conscious and subconscious thoughts running through their head. We all have them: layers of internal voices feeding us doubts, fears, and unhelpful narratives that erode our mental and physical well-being.

On average, humans have sixty thousand to eighty thousand thoughts a day. That's a lot of noise shaping how we feel, what we believe, and the choices we make; most of it is happening without us even realizing it.

Yet, despite the mind being our most powerful muscle, we were never taught how to train it. In school, we had PE (physical education) but no ME (mental education). Most of us didn't grow up with parents who knew how to teach mental strength or emotional resilience. If we want to build stronger arms, we know exactly what to do—lift weights, change our diet, or hire a trainer. But when it comes to strengthening the mind, most people are left guessing. It's not your fault; you weren't given the tools. But moving forward, you'll have them.

When I first started trying to learn how to change my thoughts after my husband left, I did what most people do…I went out and bought a few books. I started with the ones Oprah recommended: the Louise Hay, Esther Hicks, and Eckhart Tolle books on the "law of attraction" and the power of our thoughts. And I quickly felt very mentally deficient. I couldn't understand a thing they were trying to say. It felt like they talked in circles or in a foreign language that my brain couldn't comprehend or translate into practical application into my life. And no disrespect to any of those amazing thought leaders, they just didn't speak my language. I needed the concepts broken down in a way I could understand and apply.

I quickly became frustrated because everyone was saying things like, "Just think positive!" "Change your thoughts, change your life," "Positive vibes only," or "Just get in the flow." *What the fuck is "the flow"?* I thought. *What does that even mean?* The slogans and sound-bite quotes were endless, but where was the how?

I kept thinking…

But how do I think positive? Does it mean I just go around all day saying, "You're fine. Everything's fine"? Because that wasn't working; it hadn't solved any of my problems or changed how I felt.

It was like putting a Band-Aid on a bullet wound, a surface solution at best.

I wanted real answers, real solutions. I wanted to know exactly what to do and when, so that things in my life could begin to change. And so, I hacked the system. I figured out how our thoughts work on my own by breaking down the process into simple, incremental, tangible steps that anyone can understand and use to get results. I tested them, coached them, lived them, and tracked their results, both for myself and with my clients. My goal has always been to keep this simple, applicable, and results-driven. Even a child can use these tools. I've taught all three of my children, starting at a very young age, how to talk to themselves and how to change their thoughts as they've gotten older. I've witnessed the power it has given them.

And before your inner skeptic kicks in, let me say that I'm confident you've already used *Think It* throughout your life to get things you've wanted in the past—unknowingly, of course. Most people don't understand the process they've unconsciously gone through to achieve a goal or get a desired outcome; therefore, they struggle to replicate it. But when we stop to analyze any past success, we will see that it always started with a thought, also known as an idea, that we cultivated into a belief and acted upon. After reading this book, you'll have the formula, which you can cut and paste to get anything you want or to change anything you don't want.

Our thoughts create actions, and actions deliver results. This process happens automatically and is continuously creating future outcomes, both good and bad, positive and negative. The process works exactly the same either way. I realized long ago that my negative thoughts looked exactly like my reality. The correlation was impossible to ignore. Everything I'd been telling myself for years kept happening again and again in real life, which, of course, created my belief system.

A few days after my husband left, I took a long hard look at my life and asked myself a very important question: *How the fuck did I get here?* I was in line at the welfare office, crying behind my sunglasses and rolling my twins' red stroller back and forth with my foot. My son was sitting quietly next to me as we waited for our number to be called. When it was, I couldn't pull myself together long enough to tell the nice man at the counter that I needed food stamps, so he handed me a box of tissues and asked me to take a seat.

I thought, *How is this my life?* Before I'd gotten pregnant with the twins, I'd had a great job in corporate sales. We'd just bought our second home, one nicer than the first. And then it all fell apart, until there was nothing left but pieces that I was supposed to figure out how to reassemble. And I just couldn't. I couldn't think straight. Couldn't make sense of my life and what had gotten me to this point.

And that's when my quest to figure this out began.

If thoughts create reality, I wondered, does that mean I created *this?* Ouch.

That was not a pleasant realization, let me tell you. But I examined it, just for the hell of it. I started retracing some of my most obsessive thoughts over the past five years of my life. I realized I was always thinking about the worst-case scenario. I had even secretly believed that I didn't deserve my "good life" when I had it. I always worried we'd lose the house, or that I'd lose my job. I worried about money every second of every day, until it made me physically ill.

I could see now that what I'd worried about, and obsessed over, did actually happen. Repeatedly. That thought was terrifying. I looked at my other negative obsessive thoughts: my body image. Had telling myself I was hideous and that my body was disgusting (which it wasn't, by the way, but my mind was very corroded) ever helped me lose weight or get in shape? Nope. I went down the list. And it didn't take a genius to see the direct correlation between my years of negative spirals and their exact match in real life.

That was all the evidence I needed to know that this theory works. And it was enough to scare the living shit out of me! If I'd been so great at manifesting terrible outcomes with my thoughts in the past, maybe I wouldn't be half bad at manifesting better things if I could reverse the formula. I set out to figure out exactly how to do that.

Your thoughts have been shaping your reality all along—whether you realized it or not.

Unfortunately, most people use this formula backwards. Let me demonstrate what it looks like in reverse.

The Formula in Reverse: When we allow negative thoughts, they grow. When they grow, we're less motivated to take action. When we don't act, we feel like crap. When we feel crappy, we're vulnerable to depression, stagnation, stress, and anxiety. When we feel that way, we focus on it, and it grows even bigger. The bigger it gets, the more we begin to believe it as an absolute, unchangeable fact. When we believe it to be true, we will always manifest it, *making it true*. It's a vicious hamster wheel.

This is how I know you've already proven this theory in your own life. Not just because I've never met anyone who can't connect the dots when they look back at their past, but because we've all experienced self-fulfilling prophecies. And that's the same basic concept we're talking about here.

Take dating, for example. How many times have you seen a friend (or been that person) who consistently dates the same type of "wrong" person? Over time, you begin to form beliefs like, "All men (or women) are jerks!" "There are no more quality single people out there!" "Everyone is a cheater or out for themselves!" "I'm gonna be alone forever," "I'm never going to find the right partner," or "I'm not lovable or wanted," and so forth.

We can see in this example how quickly those beliefs become self-fulfilling prophecies. When my inner dialogue is telling me that I'll never find the type of partner I'm seeking and that everyone in the dating pool fits my previous experience, I can only manifest that same experience in the future. See? It's kinda crazy right? But don't worry, you're gonna learn how to change all that.

Now that you've seen how it can work in the negative, then—like me—let that *aha moment* of reflection spark a burning desire to learn how to make it work in the positive.

Personal Work

A word about the "Personal Work" sections in this book. As an elite executive mindset coach and master life coach, I know for a fact that this book will be useless if you do not do the Personal Work journaling prompts. My clients know that I'm a tough coach, but they also know I love them and want them to get results. They get those results because I don't allow them to skip this work. It's that simple. I want results for them—and for you. Period. Results are what drive everything I do as an author and a coach.

And after nearly fifteen years of coaching, teaching, and writing about my methods, I know this work has the potential to change your life forever. I have a ridiculous amount of client wins to prove it. Therefore, I am begging you…please go get a notepad and a pen…and answer these questions. This is true for every time you see "Personal Work" throughout this book. This is how you customize everything you'll learn into practical application in your own life. If you do this, I promise you'll thank me for this blunt push!

(PS If you'd rather have these questions in an actual PDF journal, you can get it for free on my website sarahcentrella.com/shop using code: READER or order the spiral-bound version.)

Take a few quiet moments to list the thoughts that show up most often in your day-to-day life. Write the answers to these questions in your journal or notepad.

- What do you find yourself constantly worried about?
- What are you obsessing over or replaying in your mind?
- What's been keeping you up at night or draining your energy?

Now dig a little deeper.

- How long do you think these thoughts have been circulating in your mind?
- Can you trace them back to a specific moment, memory, or season of your life?
- How have these thoughts shaped your emotions, your decisions, or the way you show up in your life?

Next, take an honest look at your current reality.

- In what ways does it reflect the repetitive thoughts above?
- Can you identify moments in your past when your fears or worries came to fruition?
- Can you identify any repetitive self-fulfilling prophecies in your past?

Finally, reflect on the following.

- Are you beginning to see how your internal dialogue might be writing your external story?
- How do you feel about that?

It's important to remember that this exercise is about self-discovery, not shame. You didn't know what you didn't know. You did the best you could with the tools you had at the time. If you've uncovered some patterns of negative, self-sabotaging behavior or self-fulfilling prophecies, that just means you're human. We've all been there. Every one of us has played a role in creating outcomes we didn't want. There is no shame, that's just human nature.

But now you have the tools to get this process working *for* you instead of against you. And that is very exciting.

Now that you understand how powerful your thoughts are in shaping your reality, it's time to explore the deeper layers beneath those thoughts. Next, we'll uncover how your subconscious beliefs drive your thoughts and actions. By learning where these beliefs come from and how they operate, we'll gain the clarity needed to start reshaping them in alignment with our goals. Let's dive into the root of it all: how thoughts become beliefs.

Chapter 2

How Thoughts Become Beliefs

Your Powerful Subconscious

Let's back up and talk about the origin of our deepest, most common negative thoughts—our subconscious beliefs. It took me a long time to understand the concept of embedded beliefs and why they play such a critical role in how we manifest our current reality. The incredibly frustrating thing about these beliefs is that you probably have no idea they even exist. Talk about annoying. And what's worse? They're often the opposite of what you *think* you believe. In other words, they are tricky little fuckers!

It's so important that we align our beliefs with our actions so they're both pointing in the same direction. When they're in sync, we get our desired result, often far more easily than we ever imagined. When they're in conflict or going in opposing directions, all the effort in the world won't deliver the outcome we're trying to achieve.

So, what happens when your beliefs and actions are in conflict? You can't get the results you want, because while your actions are trying to help you take a right turn, your beliefs have preprogrammed your mental GPS to take a left. When those signals are opposing each other, it's impossible to move forward, and you're stuck in the proverbial roundabout.

How Beliefs Work

The foundation for our beliefs begins when we're very young. They come from what we see and hear in our environments—at home, in the media, at school—and from the people around us. As we grow, they become solidified by the voice in our head repeating the things we've absorbed. Then we unconsciously internalize all those voices, turning them into personal labels, our identity, our "personality," and they become the story of who we are.

IRL (in real life) Example: Let's start with a simple example. Imagine that when you were five years old, you overheard your parents casually telling someone that you were "clumsy" because you tripped over your feet a few times. No big deal to them, and maybe not even to you at the time. But a few years later, your middle school basketball coach sees you trip getting off the bus and calls you clumsy in front of the whole team. Everyone laughs. Now people at school start calling you a klutz. Eventually, you adopt it as part of your identity. You start believing you're clumsy and are bound to embarrass yourself at any moment. You believe it's just who you are.

That belief now plays like a loop in your head, showing up in all kinds of moments, especially where you fear embarrassment. The thoughts say things like, *You're too clumsy to dance; you'll trip and fall,* so you don't dance at prom. Later, you're afraid to eat on a date because you might spill something down the front of your white shirt. You even start warning people by saying, "I'm such a klutz," hoping it'll soften the blow if you do something awkward. And the cycle continues, shaping your decisions and reinforcing the belief that started with an offhand comment years ago.

Okay, maybe that specific example was me, but I can't be the only one who also sat on an escalator in high school and had her shorts eaten by the disappearing stairs, requiring maintenance to turn it off and everyone in the mall to watch me get extracted from the giant moving staircase that everyone knows you're not supposed to sit on. But I digress.

A slow transformation takes place when we absorb and internalize outside opinions. And the more we think about them, wonder if they're true, or replay them in our head, the more deeply rooted they become.

Think of our beliefs as the root system of a giant oak tree. Without strong roots, the tree can't stand. Healthy roots mean a healthy tree. Our beliefs hold up the whole operation—they drive our thoughts, fuel our actions, and ultimately shape our results.

Beliefs + Thoughts + Actions = Results

How Do We Change Beliefs That No Longer Serve Us?

First, we need to identify what those beliefs are. That takes some digging and brutal honesty. Next, we need to change the thoughts that have been reinforcing those beliefs. Why? Because *repetitive thoughts create beliefs.* And consciously repeating new, empowered thoughts is how we rewire those beliefs.

But naturally, our minds might resist this change, arguing that the new thoughts aren't true and will never become true. That's okay, we don't need to believe them on day one.

Think of every time you've retold a story; how little embellishments creep in over time with each retelling. Eventually, you can't remember which parts are factual memories and which are the embellishments. It's this same principle of mental pliability that we tap into here, knowing that if you say something often enough, you'll begin to believe it.

Our brain doesn't know the difference between truth and a lie—when the lie is consistently repeated.

There are countless scientific studies that show how the brain quickly adapts and reshapes reality when we consistently tell it a new story, even if that story is a lie. (You can Google studies on neuroscience and reprogramming, or ask ChatGPT to pull some for you.) This ability is called *neuroplasticity*—the concept that "neurons that fire together wire together." In simple terms, the more we repeat a thought, the more our brain starts to accept it as truth. Over time, that repeated message replaces the original fact-based belief, and we begin to operate as if the new version is the truth.

Why wouldn't we use this existing process to our greatest advantage? This is the best brain hack; it's mental training at its finest.

And mental fitness is the ultimate form of self-care.

The more you use these positive statements and focus on the outcomes you want, the quicker you'll begin to believe them, and the faster they'll begin manifesting. Eventually, your mind will get fed up with the internal argument, and those negative thoughts will start to decrease. As they recede and the positive statement takes their place, you'll feel much more motivated to take action. The more motivated you are, the more work you'll put in. The more you hustle for what you want, the more opportunities will come your way—and the faster you'll get your desired results.

It's a simple, connected formula that you can implement to get anything you want.

Can you see how a motto or affirmation, even one that felt like a lie at first, sets off a positive domino effect? It has the power to impact motivation, actions, words, beliefs, hustle, and ultimately your results. It's so cool!

Personal Work

Take a moment to uncover your beliefs. Write down anything and everything that comes to mind about the following topics—or anything else that feels important. Be 100 percent honest. Don't filter. You can't rewire a belief you haven't identified.

- What do I believe about myself?
- What do I believe about my capabilities?
- What kind of person, parent, friend, partner, or coworker am I?
- What do I believe about money?

- What do I believe about my potential for success, happiness, or getting what I want?
- Generally speaking, what do I believe about people?
- What do I believe about God, the Universe, or my faith?
- What do I believe about love?

Now that you understand how your beliefs are formed and how they shape your reality, it's time to take the next step in our knowledge and understanding of the fundamental building blocks of *Think It*. In the next chapter, you'll be learning my revolutionary concept of mental offense and defense. Understanding this is the key to getting new results using the *Think It* tools.

Chapter 3

Mental Offense and Defense

Stop Negative Thoughts—and Start Creating New Outcomes

What is offense? What is defense? And how do we use both to stop negative thoughts and start building positive beliefs that lead to new outcomes? This concept is the revolutionary core of my trademarked mindset method, and it's the missing link in popular mindset teaching—the part no one talks about. It's a fifty-fifty equation that does two equally important jobs. It trains your thinking to proactively focus on the results you *want,* instead of continuing to create the ones you *don't.*

To achieve lasting change in your mindset, you need to implement two simple skills: the ability to play mental *offense* and *defense.*

This is why the "positivity" movement didn't work; it was simply masking the issues and not changing the source problem.

Mental Offense and Defense

Think of your mind as a basketball court or a soccer field. Whether you're a sports fan or not, you probably know that in both sports offense and defense are always in play during a game, with both teams trying to outscore and out-defend their opponent. The winning team is the one with the best offense and defense. You need both skills to win.

IRL Example: If your mind is saying, *I never have money to do the things I want to do or stay financially ahead,* here's how to play defense:

When that thought arises, think of it as the opponent trying to score. You don't just stand there, right? You try to defend the basket (your mindset). Got the visual? Great. Now, when those thoughts creep in, replace them with a motto that claims the outcome you want *instead,* like *I am providing a great life for myself and my family, more money is on its way!*

This is how we play mental *defense* to change our thoughts. We replace an old thought (one that no longer serves us) with a new one that is the opposite of the old belief and claims a new desired outcome. You'll learn several tools for this including "Mental Tennis," "I AM Statements," and "Power Mottos" in the coming chapters.

Play Offense

Several times a day, *proactively* tell yourself the story of the person you want to become and the life you want to live.

This means you're not solely playing defense. This is the key to successfully changing your thoughts, by the way. Most self-help teachings only touch on the defensive part of the equation, but without offense, we won't get new results.

By offensively thinking about your new life throughout the day, or the moments and experiences you want to live and the new outcomes you want, you're combating future negativity and speeding up its inevitable recession. You're also creating a positive, happy mental refuge from the stress of your current world. Make daydreaming a constant practice. Slip into this peaceful "happy place" as often as possible.

Over the years, I've trained my mind to go to this happy place when I'm doing mindless tasks like driving, cleaning the house, exercising, or anytime I need a quick escape. This ability to proactively focus on the life I'm creating and the moments I want to experience—rather than dwelling on the stress of daily life—has been life-changing. It's one of the fastest ways to speed up manifesting.

As you've learned in this chapter, mastering both mental offense and defense is key to transforming your thoughts and beliefs. But awareness and intention alone aren't enough; you need actionable tools to take control of the process, and that's what you'll learn in part 2.

To recap:

> Mental *Defense* is what you use in the moment when you notice you're feeling stressed, negative, or dwelling on thoughts that don't serve you.
>
> Mental *Offense* is what you use as a daily practice, putting into the Universe the outcomes you want, every day.

Next, you'll learn Mental Tennis, your first practical tool for reversing negative thoughts and replacing them with empowering beliefs. Simple yet powerful, this technique will show you how to shift your mindset in the moment, reduce stress, and pave the way for positive outcomes. It's about to get fun. Are you ready to start putting these tools into practice in your daily life?

Let's start getting mentally fit playing offense and defense on our Mental Tennis court.

Part Two

How to Change Your Mindset

The Tools

Training Your Mind with the *Think It* Tools

Now that you understand how your thoughts, beliefs, and subconscious programming are shaping your life, it's time to do something about it.

Part 2 is where we get to work. This section teaches you my seven proven mindset tools—the exact tools I've used with clients for over a decade to help them transform their lives from the inside out. These are practical, real-world strategies that train your brain to think differently in the moment, whether you're playing offense (creating what you want) or defense (stopping what you don't). This is where the rewiring happens.

Each chapter includes a "Personal Work" section that's designed to help you integrate each tool into your own life. If you skip that part, you're missing the magic. Take your time, do the work, and come back to these tools as often as you need; they're here to give you your power back.

Chapter 4

Tool #1: Snapping In

How to Take Mental Inventory

The hardest part about changing our thoughts is knowing what they are in the first place. Most of our sixty thousand-plus thoughts per day are subconscious, running like barely discernible white noise in the background. They stack on top of each other, crisscrossing and overlapping all day long.

Have you ever really tried to pay attention to your thoughts? It's intense. Ever tried to sit in silence and meditate? It's harder than it seems. Why? Because our mind is going a million miles a second, and most people can't get their inner chatter to quiet down for even a few seconds at a time, let alone reach total silence. If you've ever suffered from insomnia, you know exactly what I'm talking about: Those racing thoughts just won't let up long enough for you to fall asleep.

Let's peel back the layers of our thoughts to examine them more closely. This will help us take inventory of what we're thinking about throughout the day.

Remember, these thoughts are constantly creating our reality. So, if there's anything about your life that you want to change—any pattern, behavior, or belief—it's imperative to know what those thoughts are so you can change your future outcomes.

Conscious Thought: The Outer Layer

These thoughts consist of your to-do lists, your daily activities, your current stressors, recent conversations, mental reminders, and any consistent self-talk or ongoing anxieties. They're the manifestation of repetitive thinking, past and current actions, and underlying beliefs. These are the thoughts you focus on from day to day, and while they might seem inconsequential, they're still predicting future outcomes, impacting your emotions, and shaping your actions.

Dr. Joe Dispenza, the international best-selling author and neuroscientist, says that the average person is thinking 90 percent of the same sixty thousand thoughts from day to day. In other words, our brain recycles familiar thoughts with very little conscious involvement from us. That's pretty concerning when you realize that 90 percent of our reality is being created without our active participation. No wonder we can feel stuck in unhealthy cycles or patterns and continue to manifest them.

Subconscious Thought: The Inner Layer

Our next layer of thought consists of the subconscious, ones that run quietly in the background throughout the day. These thoughts are often harder to identify, yet they drive most of our outcomes. They can be sneaky little fuckers and are frequently linked to the deepest layer of limiting or negative beliefs.

To help us uncover this quieter inner chatter, we need to become more proactive about paying attention to our daily thoughts.

One of my favorite techniques for this is called "Snapping In." I've been teaching this simple practice to my clients for years because it's an easy way to take inventory of both your conscious and subconscious thoughts. You'll learn how to use it in just a minute.

Your Beliefs: The Core Layer

As we discussed in chapter 22, your beliefs are the root of your thoughts and outcomes. They form the core of your thought "onion," shaping your reality. That's why it's crucial to identify what you believe to be true about yourself, your abilities, your life, and your future. By uncovering these beliefs, you can change the ones that have been holding you back. But sometimes it takes a little digging to get down to the core layer. To help you understand what I mean, here's an example.

Personal Example: While I was getting ready to launch my third book, *All the Things I Wish I Knew*, I kept battling thoughts of loneliness and isolation in a post-COVID world. I even started telling myself there was no point in planning a launch event because "no one would show up anyway." These thoughts lingered on a semi-subconscious level for weeks leading up to the release—so much so that I never planned a book release party or scheduled a tour. I say "semi-conscious" because, on the surface, I was telling myself it just wasn't a good idea. It was 2021, and people still weren't gathering the way they had before the pandemic. That rationalization felt logical enough to keep me from fully committing to any kind of event, including signings, because I told myself it just "wasn't the right time."

As a result, that book had—unsurprisingly—the slowest book sales of any of my books, which was, of course, heartbreaking, considering all the work and love I'd invested in writing it and the investment my publisher had made in giving me a book deal. When I began feeling the letdown of this a few months after the book's release, I began asking myself why. *Why didn't I want to have events to promote the book's release? Why had I made that decision?* Do you see how my thoughts, both conscious (*It's just not the right time*) and subconscious (*I'm afraid no one will come*), impacted my actions (not planning any events)?

I began by examining the persistent thought or fear that no one will show up for me. I asked myself, *Why do I think that?* Well, because when I've held other events after COVID, the turnout was much lower than it was before.

Why do I think no one will ever show up for me? I asked. Other people were having events with normal turnouts, and people were eager to get together in person, so why not for me? See how that question leads to a deeper truth? I asked myself all the questions above: *When was the first example of people not showing up for me?*—and so on. Finally, I got to the root of my belief.

After tracing the origins of the belief that people would not show up for me, I came to something my mother always said when I was growing up: "People will always disappoint you; you can't count on anyone, including your family, to show up for you. You're better off on your own."

Getting to the root of this belief helped me see that my mother had influenced me in a way I was previously unaware. I could now release that limiting belief because I no longer wanted to continue manifesting her issues in my life. Not only that, but I had plenty of examples of times when people *had* shown up for me, so I began to change this limiting belief using the tools you're about to learn in the following chapters.

How to Practice Snapping In

1. **Set a Reminder**: A simple way to practice Snapping In is by setting an hourly reminder on your smartwatch, Fitbit, or phone. When it buzzes, pause and ask yourself, *What have I been thinking about for the last ten minutes? The last hour?* If possible, jot those thoughts down in your journal or send a voice memo to yourself.
2. **Log Your Thoughts**: Let's talk about why it's so important to write with pen and paper whenever possible when doing personal development work. Different parts of the brain are engaged when writing by hand versus typing on a keyboard. Research suggests that handwriting activates areas of the brain involved in memory, learning, and motor control in ways that typing does not.

When you write by hand, it engages the brain's motor cortex and involves fine motor skills. The act of forming letters and words by hand requires more cognitive processing, which strengthens neural connections, especially in areas responsible for memory, reading, and writing. This is why handwriting can improve learning and retention; it requires more focused, deliberate thought compared to typing. Handwriting tends to be more involved in the learning and retention process due to its slower pace and the intricate motor tasks involved. That's why I make all my clients do their journaling and homework with pen and paper.

However, when you're practicing Snapping In, you might be driving, walking the dog, doing the dishes, or walking to a meeting, so you can't easily write down your answers. In that case, send a voice memo to yourself listing all the thoughts you recognized in that hour. When you get home, write out the list from all your voice memos. This might seem like a lot of work, but how badly do you want to start creating new outcomes in your life? Be committed to this process for a minimum of seven days. This will give you a good idea of what you're thinking about on a daily basis. Use the same identifying method as above to asterisk the thoughts that are not serving you.

Pro Tip

One of the best ways to train yourself to practice Snapping In regularly is by setting your smartwatch to the "breathe" setting, which buzzes your wrist once an hour to remind you to breathe. If yours doesn't have this feature, set a recurring twice daily reminder to check your thoughts. Ask yourself, *What have I been thinking during the last hour?*

Another tip is tying it to daily activities, such as loading and unloading the dishwasher, doing the laundry, driving to and from work or the gym, or any other routine task. Mentally tag that activity as a reminder to take a quick inventory of your thoughts. If you do this every day for a week, you'll notice that Snapping In will begin to trigger automatically during these activities. This simple habit helps set you up for success and allows the process to run on autopilot.

Personal Work Part 1:

Write down all the topics you've noticed swirling around your mind today. Bullet them out in a quick list so you can see what's been consuming your mental space. Be specific, such as "I kept thinking about the presentation I gave at work yesterday, wishing I had done things differently," or "I was worried about covering the new bills that came today." Write until you run out of things to write.

Read through your list and put an asterisk (*) next to anything that was worry- or fear-based, stress- or anxiety-inducing, based on "lack" (for instance, "I don't have enough of *X*," or "I worry that I might not have enough"), or negative self-talk.

Now ask yourself: *Do any of these thoughts reflect something I want to manifest into reality? Do I want this thought to come true? Is this thought serving me? Is it getting me closer to the life I want?*

This exercise will help you gain clarity on the thoughts you're dealing with and the outcomes they may be creating.

Personal Work ✍ Part 2:

Review your journal entries of the thoughts you identified above, especially the ones you marked with an asterisk. For each of those thoughts, ask yourself the following questions to begin uncovering the belief behind it:

- What do I think about this topic?
- Why do I think that?
- Where does that thought come from?
- When did I first start thinking or telling myself that?
- If I think *X*, what do I believe about *X*?
- Why do I believe that?
- When did I start believing it?
- Who told me that, or where did I get this belief from?

It's totally normal if this feels difficult at first. You might draw blanks, and that's okay. These aren't questions most of us have ever taken the time to ask ourselves.

Your ongoing homework from this chapter is to daily practice Snapping In.

Chapter 5

Tool #2: Mental Tennis

The Simplest Way to Start Getting What You Want—and Stop Getting What You Don't

Offense and Defense

When I first began teaching mindset tools in 2014, one technique quickly became a favorite among my clients: Mental Tennis. Why? Because it's easy and it works. This deceptively simple tool provides a powerful way to counter the endless stream of negative thoughts that bombard you daily. With practice, you'll find that Mental Tennis can help you regain control, shift your beliefs, and create the future you've always wanted. Let's dive into how it works.

The Mental Tennis Court

Picture yourself standing on a tennis court. On the other side of the net is an automatic ball launcher firing tennis balls at you, each ball representing a negative thought. If you don't respond, you'll get hit, over and over. But if you pick up your racket and start returning the balls, you're no longer a passive recipient. Instead, you're actively engaging in the game, controlling the flow of the match and ultimately the outcome.

Every negative thought is a serve you can return. Your task is to hit the negative thought back with the positive opposite, clearly stating what you want instead.

Remember this simple three-step formula: see it, stop it, replace it.

How to Play Mental Tennis

Step 1: See It—Recognize the Thought

The first step is awareness. Pay attention to your internal dialogue using the tools you learned in Snapping In. When a thought arises that doesn't serve you, stop and acknowledge it. If thoughts become future outcomes, what outcome is it creating? Ask yourself, *Do I want this thought to become my reality?* If the answer is no, move to step two.

Step 2: Stop It—Argue with Your Thought

Just like you wouldn't sit there and absorb all those tennis balls coming your way, you can't just sit there and absorb what your head is telling you either. So, argue with the thought. You have a voice; you don't need to just be passive and take it. Speak up.

Say, *Nope. That's no longer true,* or *No thank you! I unsubscribe to that.* Or simply, *Declined.* You don't need to take every mental hit your mind tries to lob in your direction. Fight back! Make your own truth—here's how.

This is a crucial part of learning how to separate what's actually true from an old belief that no longer serves you. Just because your brain has been telling you something negative for so long that you've come to believe it doesn't make it true.

For Example: Your mind is telling you that because you didn't get a second interview for the job you wanted that you're not smart enough or good enough for that job. But that's not true. Your resume is likely proof that this is not true. So, you say, *That's not true! I am qualified for this job, and I would have crushed it, but it's clearly not the right opportunity for me, and I trust that the right one will come along.*

See how you can prevent a negative thought spiral just by challenging it?

Step 3: Replace It—Return the Serve

Ask yourself: *What is the opposite of this thought?* If the opposite doesn't immediately come to mind, ask yourself: *What do I want instead?* Most people have no idea what they want. They spend most of their time identifying and thinking about what they *don't* want. By doing this, they're actively creating undesired outcomes.

The key is to find a replacement thought that aligns with the outcome you *do* want. This process of taking the time to truly think about what you want instead is incredibly powerful. It's the first time you're identifying, declaring, and creating a new desired outcome. Once you've identified the opposite thought, repeat it to yourself after declining the negative. Say it with conviction. If possible, say it out loud. The more you repeat this new desired outcome, the faster it will manifest in your reality. In the example above, you'd say: *I am smart enough! I trust that the ideal opportunity will come to me.*

Repetition is crucial; it is how you override the old belief with the new one.

For Example:

See It: Negative thought: *I'm not good enough.*
Stop It: *Not true!*
Replace It: Positive opposite: *I am good enough. I am capable, and I'm constantly improving.*

Repetition is the magic ingredient in Mental Tennis. Say your new motto at least ten times the moment the negative thought is recognized, and every time it resurfaces. If you can, take three deep breaths while you repeat the new positive thought and imagine what it will feel like when that thought is your new reality.

What if you felt "good enough" all the time? What would that even be like? Imagine that outcome in detail and get excited by the possibility it's now creating in your life.

With repetition this new thought will start creating a new belief. When that happens, you begin showing up as the person who believes they *are* enough, and people will read and respond to that energy. The outcome you wanted is literally spoken into existence. How exciting is that? If you want even faster results, repeat that new outcome throughout the day (offense) as often as you can.

Client Example: Josh Conerly Jr. was a first-round pick in the 2025 NFL draft. In his 2024 season at the University of

Oregon, he booked a coaching session with me to see if I could help him "get out of his head" during a game or practice after making a mistake. He, like many athletes, would immediately begin beating himself up mentally after "fucking up," to the point where those fuck ups would get worse as the game or practice progressed. He, like most of us, wasn't able to "just shake it off," or "just get out of his head." And so I taught him Mental Tennis.

In a single session, I taught him exactly what to tell himself before, during, and after a game or practice to get in the most confident mental space possible using I AM Statements. And then we used Mental Tennis as soon as any negative thoughts kicked in, especially if he made a mistake. So, when his head would say something like, *Shit. You fucked up again. You always get that play wrong,* he now knew exactly what to tell himself instead. Things like *That's okay. That play is over. I got the next one. No problem. I got the next one. I'm a beast. I'm a monster. I kill this every time. Let's go, bring it on.*

So instead of negatively spiraling to a destructive headspace, he could actually redirect those thoughts into the power and motivation that focused on the outcomes he wanted and built his confidence. When I asked him if he could share his story in this book, he said, "Absolutely. I'd love to tell people how Mental Tennis helped me." This is what he said:

> Mental Tennis helped me thrive, especially in the early part of the season when we weren't playing our best ball, and there was a lot of noise and chatter about us [the Oregon Ducks football team], and most of it wasn't positive. But being able to use Mental Tennis to shake off all the negative things that were said about

us, and to knock those thoughts out of my head (for the first time ever) and not let them affect me, was something that allowed me to thrive under pressure. It helped me be more resilient and gave me the tools to not allow the negativity to affect me or let negative self-talk to kick in, even when times were rough.

It especially helped during practice. Before, if I had a bad rep or a bad period during practice, it would ruin the entire practice because I couldn't mentally shake off my mistake. But using Mental Tennis, I was able to kick out those bad thoughts and turn them into my motivation and finish practice stronger than ever.

"I hope people try Mental Tennis because if they do, it really will help."

Josh Connely Jr

Why Mental Tennis Works

Our minds are incredibly adaptable. They respond to repetition by strengthening the neural pathways associated with frequently repeated thoughts and consistent training. This means that the more you practice Mental Tennis, the stronger your positive beliefs become and the faster your negative patterns, thoughts, and beliefs begin receding, until eventually they evaporate altogether.

Visualize your negative thoughts being snuffed out the way a candle flame goes out when you put a lid on it, cutting off its oxygen. Those thoughts have only thrived in your head until now, because you gave them oxygen. You fed the flames with spiraling thoughts and negative self-talk. But now you have a tool to deprive those thoughts of oxygen and force them to die out. You're kind of a badass when you think about it.

Remember that at first, this practice will feel awkward or even fake. That's great. Do it anyway.

Examples of Mental Tennis

To help you get started, here are some common negative thoughts and their empowering positive opposites to help you begin practicing this tool on your own thoughts starting today.

Negative thought: *Other people do it better.*
Positive opposite: *I am good at this. I am getting better every day.*

Negative thought: *I'm so tired.*
Positive opposite: *I feel great, full of energy.*

Negative thought: *Everyone else has a partner but me, I'll never find love.*
Positive opposite: *I am loved. I am loveable. My great love is on the way!*

Negative thought: *What if I fail?*
Positive opposite: *What if I succeed?*

Negative thought: *FML. (fuck my life.)*
Positive opposite: *LML! (love my life!)*

Negative thought: *I'm overwhelmed.*
Positive opposite: *I get shit done, one thing at a time. I got this!*

Negative thought: *I suck at XYZ.*
Positive opposite: *I'm good at XYZ. I'm always improving.*

Negative thought: (*Any negative money thought.*)
Positive opposite: *I am already abundant now!*

Negative thought: *Something bad is going to happen.*
Positive opposite: *I am safe. Good things always happen to me.*

Negative thought: *My job sucks.*
Positive opposite: *I am grateful for my job.*

Get the picture? Our assignment is to identify and claim the new outcome, even if it feels like a complete lie.

Speak the new outcome into existence. All day, every day.

Now that you've identified the empowering thoughts, these statements become your mantras. Each time the negative thought arises, respond with the new opposite. Over time, these affirmations and mantras will begin to rewire your mindset.

Pro Tip

Always claim the outcome you want by saying "I am," instead of "I want," or "I will." Declare it as if that outcome is already your current reality.

Client Example: On our coaching call one week, my client Nikaya shared a powerful win that's too good not to pass along, because it's such a real, in-the-moment example of how Mental Tennis *actually works* in your everyday life.

Nikaya is a college student who's been working with me to shift out of anxiety and self-doubt and into confidence and belief in herself. She'd been applying for summer jobs for weeks with no luck. A few interviews, no offers, and then the negative thoughts crept in: *Maybe I'm just not going to get a job. Maybe I'm not as qualified as other people.*

But here's where it clicked. She *caught* that thought spiral—mid-spin—and snapped into Mental Tennis. She responded with

Screw that! I'm a great worker. I'm smart. I've got experience. There's no way I won't get a job this summer. I'm getting a full-time job, Monday through Friday, and I'm going to love it!

Within hours, she got a call for an interview from a job she'd applied to earlier. On her way there, she stayed in offense mode, telling herself: *You're perfect for this job. They're going to love you. This job is fun, great for your resume; they'd be crazy not to hire you.*

She *nailed* the interview. But she didn't stop there. She kept her inner dialogue focused on the outcome she wanted using these tools. The next day, she felt so confident and excited about the job that she called the manager to express how much she wanted it. That follow-up impressed the manager so much, she was offered the job on the spot!

That's what happens when you train your thoughts. When you learn how to talk to yourself to build your confidence instead of letting your mind tear you down, you take inspired action. If she'd stayed in self-doubt, none of that would've happened. She wouldn't have shown up with that confident energy, wouldn't have followed up, and likely wouldn't have gotten the job. But she didn't let the spiral win—she used her tools, and she manifested the outcome she wanted, the one in-line with her new empowered mindset and beliefs.

Pro Tip #1: Surround Yourself with Mottos

Write your mottos on sticky notes and place them where you'll see them: your bathroom mirror, your desk, or even your car dashboard. Record them as voice memos on your phone and listen to them several times a day. The more you see and hear them, the faster they'll take root. This is an example of how you practice "offense." In other words, you are offensively and actively adding these thoughts to your daily life on a consistent basis.

Pro Tip #2: Practice, Even When It Feels Fake

It's normal for these new thoughts to feel untrue at first. They should! If you're doing the assignment correctly, they will be the direct opposite of what you've been telling yourself for years—and of what you currently believe—so of course they feel like a complete lie. If they don't, then you haven't found the true positive opposite. Remember, the more you repeat them, the less resistance your mind will produce. So, just do it.

Pro Tip #3: Proactively Use Your New Mottos Throughout the Day

Don't wait for a negative thought to arise. Proactively repeat your mottos during mindless tasks like driving, cleaning, or exercising. This consistency accelerates the brain-training process.

Personal Work ✍

Take out your journal and reflect on these prompts: Write down five recurring negative thoughts you've noticed. For each thought, identify the positive opposite that you want instead. Practice repeating each new motto ten times daily.

For example:

Negative thought: *I'll never achieve my goals.*
Positive opposite: *I will achieve my goals.*

Negative thought: *I can't do this.*
Positive opposite: *I can do it; I am strong.*

As you've learned in this chapter, Mental Tennis is a simple yet transformative tool for reversing negative thoughts and building empowering beliefs that create new desired outcomes. By consistently practicing this technique, you'll begin to create a life that aligns with your deepest desires. It's time to start returning those serves: Do the work above. You've got this!

Chapter 6

Tool #3: I AM Statements

How to Reprogram Your Identity to Become the Next Best Version of You

Offense

I first learned about this concept on *The Oprah Winfrey Show* back in the early 2000s when Joel Osteen was her guest. Now, I'm not a religious person (read my memoir *Anomaly*, and you'll understand why), so at first, I was resistant to the concept based on the messenger. But I decided to approach it with an open mind, and I encourage you to do the same. He gave a sermon on the power of "I am" and wrote a book about it if you'd like to dig deeper into that perspective. I listened to the sermon, and I gotta say, it shook me. The concept is so simple that you immediately want to dismiss it as "too easy to be true," but I promise that would be a mistake. Because though it is indeed basic, it is insanely powerful.

This is the general idea…

Any time we say the words "I am" followed by a descriptive word, we are labeling ourselves that thing. We are declaring it to be true.

And whenever we declare something and constantly repeat it, we begin believing it as if it were a fact. Once we believe it, we make it so.

That being true, think of all the times throughout the day we label ourselves with things we do *not* want to be! We say things like, "I am tired," "I am overwhelmed," or even "I am stupid." Are these things we want to be? Are they making our day better when we mentally or verbally repeat them? Or are they making it harder to find our energy because we've spent the day saying how tired we are? Does telling ourselves constantly that we're overwhelmed make us feel more organized and in control of our life? Are we unknowingly passing on opportunities because we were casually labeling ourselves as not smart enough?

Think about all the self-critical thoughts you have or the self-deprecating things you say. I bet the words "I am" precede many of those. If so, it's time to change that.

Test the Power of Your Thoughts at the Gym or a Workout

There's no better place to test how much your thoughts affect your reality than at the gym. If you're even a little skeptical about the idea that what you think influences your reality, try this experiment.

Remember that this concept works whether you're thinking positively or negatively. So, run both sides of this test to collect your own proof points.

Part One

Decide you're going to work out twice this week. Pick your two days. On day one, intentionally talk down to yourself. Say things like, *Ugh, I don't want to do this. I'm so tired. This is pointless. I don't have the energy. I hate the gym.* And then go anyway.

When you get there, keep it going: *This sucks. Everything hurts. I'm not into this today.*

Now pay attention: How did your body feel during that workout? How was your energy level? How motivated were you? What was that experience like? Did you have a good workout?

Part Two

On your next workout day, flip the script. Wake up and say: *I feel amazing! I'm excited to work out today. I love how strong my body is. I have so much energy today!*

And during the workout, tell yourself: *I'm powerful. This is easy. My body is crushing this. I feel strong, fit, and energized.*

Then notice: How did *that* workout feel? How did your body respond? Was there a noticeable difference between the two days?

Now you have your answer. Real data from your own experience. Same body. Same workout. Different thoughts. Different outcome.

That's how powerful your thoughts are. That's why learning how to train your thinking will change your entire life.

Client Example: Meet Jennifer, a client who struggled with chronic self-doubt. She often thought, *I'm not smart enough to advance in my career.* Using Mental Tennis, she identified the opposite thought: *I have the skills and intelligence to thrive in my career, my voice is needed and valued.* At first, this felt untrue, but she stuck with it. Every time the negative thought surfaced, she repeated the positive one ten times. She then used her I AM Statements and said things like *I am smart, I am successful, I am valued*, and *I am intelligent.* She said these throughout the day as often as possible, faithfully every day.

Within weeks, Jennifer noticed a shift. She started volunteering for new projects at work, and her confidence grew. Months later, she landed a promotion she once thought was out of reach. Not long after that, she was chosen for a very prestigious leadership retreat, one she'd previously believed was exclusively reserved for "smart" people. When she told me about her wins, I said, "See? You are smart! It was always factual, but now you truly believe it."

Her transformation began the moment she made the commitment to practice these tools every day. After her retreat, she told me how she'd sat at the table with the senior executives and felt completely comfortable. Her voice was needed and valued in the conversation, just like she'd always dreamed it would be.

Her I AM Statements helped her build internal confidence, which began changing the energy she put out into the world and at her job. People began responding to that new energy and elevating her in new ways. Her actions changed to support these new beliefs, and now she genuinely feels comfortable and valued in her role and eager to take on new challenges.

This wasn't magic or "fake it till you make it"—this was her actively changing who she is and how she operates by first changing her internal dialogue.

How to Write Effective I AM Statements

Step 1: This List Should Be Entirely Aspirational

In other words, none of the items on your list should describe who you are *right now*; they should all be who you *want to become.*

Step 2: They Should Feel Like a Lie

Right now, everything you write down will be the opposite of how you genuinely feel, so this will seem "fake." That's okay. That's exactly what we want, because we are using this tool to create the *next* version of ourselves. This is the power of I AM Statements; they declare that you are *already* who you aspire to be. They claim a future desired outcome as if it was your current reality. Speak it into existence.

Step 3: Each Statement Should Have Only One Word Following "I Am"

For example: "I am successful."

The simplicity of these statements is their genius. Because they're so short, they are easy to commit to memory, especially after saying them out loud twice a day for thirty days. Soon they will start to organically influence your decisions. Now instead of automatically acting on the old belief, you'll have two voices in your head: one from your past narrative, and the other will be your new I AM Statement, giving you the opportunity to choose a new outcome.

Now you'll have a clear decision to make: Do I continue doing what I've always done, or am I committed to taking new actions to back up this I AM Statement?

It's crazy how effective these little affirmations are at reminding and encouraging us to take new action. When you make a new decision, your transformation has begun. Soon that statement will begin morphing into your new identity and become your reality. It still blows my mind every time someone experiences this transformation for the first time. It's so fucking insane how pliable our mind is and how quickly this training helps us become the next best version of ourselves.

The Mirror Exercise

Because I AM Statements are an *offensive* tool, we need to be proactive about creating a daily practice to implement them. This is an exercise I've had all my clients do for the past decade when coaching my Centrella Method, and it's unbelievably effective.

First, commit to saying them **out loud** to yourself in the mirror every morning and night, **for thirty days.**

Second, it's important that you **keep eye contact** with yourself in the mirror when you speak these words out loud. When you do this, you'll notice a powerful reaction. It will probably feel uncomfortable, awkward, and even silly. It could also be difficult: Maybe your throat tightens when you say certain positive statements, the words might literally be hard to speak. If that happens, just know that you've touched on a block or limiting belief, which is a very good thing. This makes it easier for us to identify beliefs that have previously held us back. It could also be emotional. If so, pay attention to which I AM Statements bring up these feelings, because it's those sticky ones that do the deepest work.

This thirty-day practice is a critical element to getting the maximum benefit from this work. If you commit to it, you'll be surprised by how quickly things start to shift—sometimes in just a week's time. But don't get lazy and stop doing it once you start feeling good. Keep the daily practice going so you can continue creating magic in your life.

Personal Work

Grab your journal and write out twenty-five positive I AM Statements. These questions will help you curate a list that is customized to you and accurately describes the personal transformation you wish to create. Ask yourself:

- Who do I *want to be*?
- How do I want to be *treated* (by bosses, coworkers, my partner, my kids, and all the people in my life)?
- How do I want to *feel* (about myself, my life, my various roles in life)?
- Who do I want to *become* (what words describe the next version of me)?
- What do I want to *believe* (about myself, my life, my capabilities)?

After answering the above questions, you should have a list of around twenty-five positive I AM Statements. Be sure to do your daily mirror practice. A great way to remember is to do this before or after you brush your teeth, first thing in the morning and last thing before bed. This will help you mentally tie brushing your teeth with saying your I AM Statements. This helps the habit stick.

By committing to these positive affirmations, you are setting the stage for massive ongoing transformation.

Now you know how to use one of the most powerful tools for reshaping your beliefs, shifting your mindset, and transforming your reality. This simple daily practice helps you declare who you are becoming, rather than reinforcing who you've always been. Keep pushing through any discomfort you feel when speaking these declarations aloud until they loosen enough for you to let them go.

As you continue to practice this over the next thirty days, you'll start to notice subtle but profound changes in how you show up in the world and how people respond to you. Your energy will be shifting each day into a more empowered place where momentum begins to build. Your confidence will start growing, and the people in your life will feel that shift. Not everyone will appreciate this new improved version of you, and that's okay. You are not changing for them, you are making very intentional shifts in yourself and your life, for *you*. Stand in that truth and be proud of your progress whether others applaud you or not.

Pro Tip #1

After the first thirty days, do a quick audit of your twenty-five statements. Are there any that you've outgrown or no longer need? Ask yourself if some no longer resonate. Have your beliefs shifted? Over time, you'll *become* the things you've been affirming, so once a statement goes from feeling like a "lie" to resonating truthfully, you don't need to keep repeating it. Remove any affirmations that have evolved into positive beliefs and replace them with your next level of desired transformation, or any new items you'd like to work on.

Pro Tip #2

Head to YouTube and search for free guided I AM meditations. There are tons to choose from, so pick one that aligns with what you're working on that day—whether it's building confidence, attracting abundance, or cultivating success.

They're especially powerful to play right before bed or first thing in the morning. I personally hit play about fifteen minutes before I need to get up. It sets the tone for my day and works on rewiring my subconscious during those highly receptive moments right before and after sleep.

Chapter 7

Tool #4: Power of Pause

How to Quickly Reduce Stress or Anxiety in Real Time

Defense

Anxiety doesn't always start as a full-blown panic attack. It often begins with a single thought, one that *feels true* but often is not. In this chapter, we're going to focus on one of the hardest thought patterns to shift: "the stressors." These are deeply ingrained, often subconscious narratives that can instantly trigger fear, anxiety, stress, or even panic. They're built over time, layered with self-made "facts" through repeated experiences and self-fulfilling prophecies, making them feel unshakable.

In my coaching practice, I work with clients every day who are navigating anxiety at various levels, and I've seen how pervasive it's become. We live in a fear-based world, where it's nearly impossible to avoid the constant stream of negativity, crisis, and uncertainty. Over time, that external noise turns into internal stories—stories that keep our nervous system on high alert and make us feel like danger is always around the corner. According to the American Psychiatric Association's 2024 poll, 43 percent of adults reported feeling more anxious than the previous year, a steady increase from 37 percent in 2023 and 32 percent in 2022. This growing trend is impacting people across all demographics and is quickly becoming one of the most urgent threats to our mental well-being.

I've worked with several clients who've reached severe stages of anxiety-related disorders, including agoraphobia. Agoraphobia is an intense fear of situations where escape might be difficult or where help might not be available if a panic attack or other distressing symptoms occurs. This fear often leads to avoiding certain places or situations, severely disrupting daily life.

Client Example: One of my clients developed sudden-onset agoraphobia and became absolutely petrified to drive. Just sitting at a stoplight would trigger a full-blown panic attack. We worked together to retrain her thinking around driving, replacing the fear-based thoughts that were fueling her anxiety with new ones that built confidence and shifted her entire relationship with driving. I know it sounds wild, but it worked.

Every day, she repeated a new Power Motto:

I love to drive! Driving gives me freedom and
is so empowering because I know I am safe.
Being stopped in traffic gives me a chance
to be grateful and make someone smile.

She's a classically trained dancer, so I gave her a challenge: Whenever she was stopped in traffic, she should crank up her favorite music and have a little car dance party. It was just for herself, but also to see if she could get the person next to her to smile. She loved that idea and jumped right in. We put those mottos around her house and right by the door, so they were the last thing she saw before getting in the car. We also used the Power of Pause to stop the spiral of anxious thoughts whenever they arose, giving her a chance to regulate before intrusive thoughts took over.

Just one week into using these tools, she came to our session with a huge win, one that gave me goosebumps. She said, "For the first time in almost two years, I drove without fear. I actually felt excited and free." And yes, she even got a stranger in the car next to her to start dancing at a red light. Changing the core thoughts and beliefs stopped her anxiety and panic attacks and got her back out doing things she loved. Our mind is so powerful!

I've had clients who haven't left their homes in years, people who, before developing severe anxiety, lived what most would consider "normal" lives. Many come to me after they've tried everything else—therapy, medication, you name it—but nothing has helped them return to that sense of normalcy. This is where I've seen the most dramatic results from using the Power of Pause.

I've also worked with clients who experience frequent panic attacks, social anxiety disorder, or other forms of anxious behavior. And the tool we consistently use to help interrupt and manage the thoughts that fuel anxiety is the Power of Pause. If you're willing to commit to practicing it regularly, it *will* work for you too.

Though I'm a believer in traditional methods for addressing anxiety—such as therapy, medication (when needed), homeopathic medicine, and other forms of treatment—none of those address the core cause of anxiety: the thoughts that lead to the fear in the first place.

If we are only addressing anxiety through the common methods of calming the physiological response, numbing our responses through medication or simply trying to reframe the perceptions of a threat, we are missing the core issue.

Anxiety often arises from a combination of thoughts and triggered threats, whether they're perceived or real. Thoughts like anticipatory thinking, negative self-talk, and unresolved worries play a major role. For example, anxiety can stem from worst-case-scenario thinking about the future or a constant inner dialogue that focuses on failure and inadequacy. Repetitive thoughts about unresolved issues, such as financial stress or relationship problems, can also serve as significant triggers.

Often, anxiety creates a feedback loop where encountering a perceived threat leads to anxious thoughts, and repeated negative thinking reinforces the brain's perception of danger, even in non-threatening situations. This is why it's crucial to address the thoughts that are causing the anxiety.

Personal Example: For years, I was afraid of flying. As you might imagine, this was highly problematic for someone as obsessed with travel as I am and someone who travels for work as much as I do. This fear began after watching the planes hit the Twin Towers on 9/11. I started giving mental space to stories in my head that transferred what I saw on television—the stories of people on those planes—into "what ifs" in my own life. "What if that was me on that flight? That could have been me." I'm sure you're familiar with this general line of thinking and have experienced it in some form in your own life.

The problem was that I couldn't stop this narrative from playing out those scenarios in my mind, especially when I knew I had to fly. For years, I needed to numb my nerves with a glass of wine or a quick airport cocktail just to get on the flight and avoid having a panic attack. Every bump or spot of turbulence instantly triggered those doomsday thoughts. My heart would race, my mind would panic, and I'd imagine the plane going down. It was horrible. I knew I couldn't continue to live like this.

So, I began applying the Power of Pause. When the thoughts would surface before a trip, I'd first tell myself, *Listen, there's nothing I can do about it right now, so I choose not to go there. I'm going to have a safe and enjoyable flight!* (putting the thought on pause). Then I began training my mind to instantly change the subject. I did this by imagining things I was excited to do once I arrived at my destination or daydreaming about anything that felt exciting at the time. This redirection helped the thoughts of fear and panic get quieter and become less effective over time.

Next, I started changing that mental story by telling myself—any time the thought of flying came up—*I love to fly! I love the freedom flying affords me. It's so safe and relaxing. I fly like a boss! Takeoffs and landings are my favorite.* I'd repeat these mantras consistently, shifting the narrative and focusing on the outcome I wanted.

Lastly, I created a new routine around flying. I began dressing for success when I traveled so I'd feel good and carry myself with confidence. I'd repeat my mantras as I boarded the flight, put on some of my favorite music, and distract myself during takeoff and landing by playing a mindless game like Farm Crush.

It took a while, but I'm no longer afraid to fly. In fact, I genuinely *love* it now. I use that time to journal, reflect, or read, activities that feel restorative and relaxing. And best of all, I no longer freakout or need a buzz to get on a flight.

When negative thoughts arise, they can feel relentless, like they demand your immediate attention. Telling yourself to simply "stop thinking about it" often backfires, creating even more stress. That's why the Power of Pause is such an effective tool. It's not about dismissing your thoughts altogether; it's about learning how to stop obsessive, negative thinking.

Most problems that trigger stress can't be solved in the moment, especially not in the million moments a day they pop into your mind. Our mind craves resolution, but giving attention to stressors every time they show up doesn't solve anything. The Power of Pause interrupts that loop.

How to Use the Power of Pause

Step 1: Recognize the Thought

When a negative thought surfaces, don't ignore it. Acknowledge it. Say, "Okay, I get it, that's stressful. But I don't want to manifest that outcome." This stops the resistance and helps prevent spiraling.

Step 2: Pause the Thought

Train yourself to stop obsessing when there's nothing you can do about it *right now*. Ask: "Is there anything I can do *right now* to change this?" If not, stop the thought before it manifests. Say, "Thinking about this is creating what I don't want. I can't afford that, so I'm choosing to stop thinking about *X* right now."

Step 3: Agree to Address the Issue

Set aside time to actually address the issue. Stressful thoughts are persistent because they're asking to be solved. They are reminding us of a problem (real or perceived) that needs our attention. Don't ignore them; schedule time to deal with them. Let's say your stressor is money related. You say: "I can't change this right now, so I refuse to keep obsessing. I'll sit down Sunday morning and flush out some options."

Then, on Sunday morning, you grab your coffee and face your issues head-on. This focused action quiets that anxious voice triggered by procrastination. Next time that stressor pops up, just go back and repeat steps one and two of the Power of Pause. Step three is one you shouldn't have to do more than once or twice—simply remind yourself that *I already sat down and tried to solve it, and I'm actively doing everything I can to improve my situation.* Then move to step four below.

Step 4: Change the Subject

Once you've paused the thought, redirect your focus. Use a quick bait-and-switch with yourself to replace the spiral with something joyful or exciting. For me, that means mentally planning a dream trip or imagining the big moments I'm actively working toward achieving. This shift is what starts creating a future you *do* want and stops creating the cycle you don't.

Why the Power of Pause Is So Effective

The Power of Pause works because it taps into the strength of compartmentalization, a powerful mental strategy that can completely transform how you manage stress, emotions, and challenges. One of its biggest benefits is the ability to reduce overwhelm. By setting clear boundaries around when and how you'll engage with stressful thoughts, you create a buffer between yourself and the chaos of constant worry. Choosing to pause and compartmentalize prevents anxious thoughts from consuming your entire day, stops them from manifesting negative outcomes, and helps you feel more in control.

So, if I'm obsessing over my bills while I'm stuck in traffic or on the treadmill, how is that solving the problem or adding more money to my bank account? It's not. But what it *is* doing is manifesting more future bills and less future money, two things I definitely don't want.

The Power of Pause teaches us how to interrupt those thoughts in the moment, stopping that negative loop and helping us avoid manifesting what we don't want, especially in situations where we have no power to fix it right then anyway.

Another significant benefit of the Power of Pause is how it supports effective problem-solving. When you set aside specific times to think through challenges, you're able to approach them with more clarity and focus. Instead of letting problems swirl around in your mind—or trying to ignore them entirely—this tool gives you a structured way to engage with them intentionally. By creating space for focused thinking, you reduce mental noise and increase your ability to find real, workable solutions.

Lastly, this tool helps protect your energy. By compartmentalizing negative thoughts, you free up valuable mental space that can be redirected toward more positive thoughts and productive actions. Rather than letting negativity drain your energy, you can shift your focus to something that brings you joy, boosting both your well-being and productivity.

Remember, this process is a journey and a daily practice, one you'll get better at with repetition. It takes time to build the habit of pausing and redirecting your thoughts. If it feels hard at first, that's okay. Be kind to yourself. Recognize how far you've already come by picking up this book and committing to change—that's a big step. The more you practice, the easier it will become, and the payoff is life-changing.

Personal Work

1. Write down the top five things in your life that trigger your stress and anxiety. Is it your health? Your finances? Your relationships? Identify the areas that need your attention.
2. Why do they trigger stress or anxiety? What is the root fear associated with each stressor?
3. For each of these five stressors, write down how you *wish* you felt about each one, in other words, what do you want instead? Write it in the present tense claiming desired outcome. For example: If you stress about not having enough money, write "I have more than enough money to pay my bills on time, enjoy my life, and plan for my future."
4. During your scheduled thinking time, give the stressor your full attention. Brainstorm solutions, write about them, or devise a plan to address the issue. Once your time is up, imagine locking this "problem" up in a box and going about your day, thinking about things that make you happy.

Whenever the negative thoughts resurface, restate the identified outcome you want instead. Remind yourself that there is nothing you can do about it right now, so you are choosing to no longer give this issue your attention. Then change the subject in your mind, go to your mental "happy place." Imagining the day when this problem or trigger no longer exists.

As you begin practicing the Power of Pause, you'll experience immediate relief and begin to see the long-term benefits of redirecting your focus. By consistently applying this tool, your stress and anxiety triggers will diminish, and you'll begin believing the new desired outcome is on its way.

In the next chapter, we'll dig a little deeper into creating Power Mottos for our top stressors to help us change those negative and limiting beliefs quickly and give us a shot of empowerment when we need it most.

Chapter 8

Tool #5: Power Mottos

How to Rewire Your Beliefs, Feel Empowered, and Create New Outcomes

Offense and Defense

Mottos, mantras, and affirmations aren't new, but the way we will create and use them is. The concept of a "motto" has been around for thousands of years, used by cultures across the globe as tools for focus, motivation, and transformation. Ancient Indian traditions introduced mantras like "om" to center the mind and connect to something greater. Buddhist chants were designed to purify the mind and bring peace. Even mottos like "carpe diem" (seize the day) from ancient Rome or knightly slogans from medieval Europe served as guiding principles. Even rapper and singer Drake made YOLO (you only live once) a motto anthem that helped launch his career. Today, we use these same powerful tools in a fresh way: to rewire our thinking, replace negative beliefs with empowering ones, and intentionally shape our future.

Trying to stop negative thinking by repeating generic mantras like "everything's going to be okay" or "it'll all work out" is useless. The problem with this approach is that it does not create a new outcome.

Think of your thoughts as cars traveling a road full of roundabouts. If you, the driver, don't know how to navigate roundabouts, you'll end up stuck, going in circles all day long. Without an activated GPS to instruct you on which off-ramp to take, you'll never get to your destination. But what happens when you set the navigation to the exact location where you want to go? You get clear directions, instructing you on the correct route to take each time you approach a roundabout. That guidance is essential; you need to create the road ahead if you ever expect to reach your destination.

That's exactly what happens in our mind when we keep recycling old thoughts without giving our brain new outcomes to focus on. How could we ever expect to get what we want when our mental GPS is programmed to focus on what we don't want, sending us around the same loop over and over? The moment we proactively input thoughts of what we *do* want, we begin creating a mental roadmap to our desired result.

One of the fastest and easiest ways to change what you think, feel, and believe is by using Power Mottos and I AM Statements. I use mottos for any recurring negative thoughts, especially those I find myself stressing or obsessing over most often. They're quick to commit to memory and incredibly effective for changing beliefs and creating new outcomes.

How to Write a Power Motto

A good Power Motto has a few crucial elements that make it effective:

Step 1: Acknowledge the Thought – What's the Stressor?

We start by acknowledging the original thought and identifying the stressor. *What is stressing you out?* Then we need to understand the core reason behind the thought: What is causing it? If the stress is fear-based, what is the true fear? If it's rooted in lack, what are you lacking? Why does that thought cause stress or trigger anxiety?

Step 2: Identify the Best-Case Scenario

What do you want *instead?* How do you want to feel? What is your desired outcome? What's the best-case scenario? What is the opposite of that stress?

Step 3: Focus on Gratitude

What can you be grateful for right now, in relation to this topic?

Step 4: Finish With a Power Statement

End your Power Motto by claiming this new outcome as your truth. Choose a statement that feels powerful and gives you hope every time you say it.

Say this new Power Motto to yourself at least ten times a day; repeat it until it's committed to memory. Do this every day, until you no longer need it because you've transformed *into it.* Say it in the morning when you wake up. Say it while you're driving or walking the dog. Repeat it as often as possible. This is the "offense" part of the program. You are intentionally putting this new statement out into the Universe as often as you can.

This also works as "defense" because when the triggering thought arises, these new mottos will start to kick in automatically to counter or argue with the old thoughts or beliefs. This is the double power of a great Power Motto.

The more you repeat it, the better you'll feel, and the faster those stressful thoughts will recede. It might sound too simple to be true, but trust me, it works.

It's incredibly powerful, and it has delivered results for every client I've ever coached. If you're committed to a regular practice, it will work for you too.

An Example of Controlling Negative Thoughts About Health

If you've been spiraling about a health issue, ask yourself: *What is my deepest worry or fear as it relates to my health? Why are these stressful or negative thoughts coming up? What am I really afraid of?*

Now, ask yourself: *What is the opposite of that? How would I feel if I were healthy, vibrant, and felt amazing? What if everything I'm worried about turned out to be okay?*

Maybe it's something completely out of your control. Maybe you're dealing with a terrifying health diagnosis, facing something difficult, or simply feeling generally worried. But no matter the situation, our *mindset* is always the one thing we can control. So really, what's the downside of putting the best-case scenario out into the Universe? What harm is there in feeding your mind and body a little optimism?

There is overwhelming evidence that your mind can heal your body, so why *not* buy in?

Research has increasingly demonstrated the profound connection between the mind and body, highlighting how mental processes influence physical health. Mind-body therapies, such as meditation, mindfulness (what we're practicing in *Think It*), and yoga, have been shown to reduce stress, decrease anxiety, and enhance overall well-being. Mindfulness meditation can lead to changes in brain plasticity, affecting neural transmissions in ways that support health benefits.

The placebo effect further illustrates the mind's capacity to influence healing. Believing in the efficacy of a treatment—even if it's inactive—can lead to real physiological improvements. This phenomenon underscores the power of mindset and expectations in shaping health outcomes.

Incorporating mind-body practices into healthcare can foster resilience and improve the management of chronic pain and stress-related conditions. Research has proven that by leveraging the mind's influence over the body, you can enhance your overall health and well-being. (If you'd like to see research behind these concepts, just ask Google or ChatGPT to pull studies showing the mind body connection, neuroplasticity, the health benefits of calming the mind, and how the placebo effect happens.)

Now let's create a Power Motto to help align your mind with your body to get the results you want. Start with a statement that identifies the best-case scenario, the opposite of your greatest fear. Something like: *I am healing,* or *I am getting healthier every day.* Next, choose a statement that resonates with you, one that feels powerful and claims the outcome you want while incorporating gratitude: *I am grateful for my health, my body is responding quickly, and I feel better every day.*

Remember, your motto is designed to help create the reality you want, so give that your undivided focus.

Financial Stress Example

First, ask yourself: *What am I really afraid of when it comes to finances? What's the deep, underlying fear? Where does that sense of lack come from?* Let's say you uncover that your fear is rooted in not being able to provide for your family. You want the Power Motto to be strong enough to eradicate this fear without giving it power.

The first part of your motto might be: "I am providing a beautiful life for my family." This statement acknowledges the fear but reframes it into something empowering while claiming the outcome you want.

The next part of the motto expresses gratitude for what you have now, and the last part needs to pack a punch, planting the belief that change is possible. It could say: "I am grateful for all I have and eagerly anticipate the abundance that is to come!"

The new money motto might be something like this:

"I am blessed to provide a beautiful life for myself and my family. I am grateful for all I have and eagerly anticipate the abundance that is to come!"

This becomes the statement you repeat daily until it is committed to memory and auto-populates in your mind, contradicting old thoughts of lack whenever they arise.

This motto rewrites your deepest beliefs of lack in a way that inspires hope and confidence. It shows gratitude for what you already have while building expectancy for the abundance to come. When you say it consistently, it begins to shift how you feel about money. You start noticing signs of improvement, feeling more grateful for what you do have, and gratitude is one of the fastest ways to expedite abundance manifestations.

You begin to feel thankful each time you pay a bill, sending up a small prayer of gratitude for being able to provide for your family. Your perspective starts to shift, and as that perspective changes, the world around you moves into alignment with this new belief, creating a new reality to match.

But I can hear you saying, "Yeah right. How is saying my Power Motto all day going to result in more money being deposited into my bank account?" All I can say is that it will. It *will.* It has for me for nearly fifteen years, it has for my clients, and it will for you—if you do this work and are consistent. How? Because it rewrites the belief and a belief will always become self-fulfilling.

Soon you'll notice that opportunities start coming into your life, maybe you get a raise at work or a promotion. Maybe you meet a person that becomes a new business partner, or you're offered a new job with a bigger salary. You could get a surprising discount on something you expected to pay full price for. You could have a new idea that results in either money being saved or more coming in. There are endless ways that abundance will start showing up in your life once your thoughts, focus, and beliefs begin to change.

Remember those old-school tape deck players from the '90s? Okay, I'm aging myself here, but back in high school, we'd sit by the radio for hours, waiting for our favorite song to come on. The second it did, we'd slam a blank cassette into the deck and hit *record*—wiping out whatever was on the tape before, excited to capture the hottest new track. (If that just brought back a forgotten happy memory, you're welcome! And if you're too young to get the reference…I'm sorry, it was a whole vibe that you missed out on.)

Anyway, that's exactly what we're doing here, acknowledging that while there may have been songs we once loved on that old tape, we've outgrown them. We want the new track more than the familiar mix. Rewriting beliefs works the same way: We recognize that the old ones no longer serve us and consciously choose the new, because they reflect the future we're creating. So, when the old "lack" narrative starts to play, we stop the tape and listen to the new version instead.

"I am already abundant now!"

Personal Example: I remember in early 2020, when the pandemic hit and business slowed down overnight. So many of my in-person speaking gigs were canceled all at once, and I found myself slipping back into old habits. I was stressing about money and worrying how I'd continue providing for my family. I had worked so hard to build a business that was not only stable but thriving, and suddenly, through no fault of my own, I was back in a financially vulnerable place.

It brought up deep familiar fears. Fears I'd carried since childhood about not having enough and struggling to make ends meet. As a self-employed single mom responsible for a family of four, that kind of uncertainty can feel overwhelming and terrifying. Even though I've been practicing these mindset tools for over fifteen years, I'm human and, like anyone else, can slip into negative thought patterns. When life hits hard, I can get caught in the stress without even realizing my focus has shifted. That's why it's important for me to pay attention to how I *feel*. If I notice that I've started feeling shitty, anxious, stressed, or moody, that's my indicator that I've let my mental practice slip and it's time to start using my tools in earnest.

I know I'm a powerful manifester. That's both a blessing and a curse, because I can turn my thoughts into reality fast—sometimes in just a few days. And if those thoughts are rooted in stress or lack, I can quickly fuck myself. Therefore, the moment I catch myself focusing on the negative, I must immediately snap out of it and shift. If I don't, I risk attracting exactly what I don't want.

The truth is, I'm not naturally a super-positive person. That's why I lean on these tools. They hold me accountable and help me course-correct when I'm slipping. I trust them. They've pulled me out of some dark places and tough situations. I know that if I choose to use them, they'll stop the downward spiral and get things moving in the right direction again.

In these situations, I make myself double down on my Power Mottos. I listen to my abundance meditations every day and use my I AM Statements to rebuild faith in my ability to once again manifest financial abundance. Back in early 2020, after all my planned events were canceled, I had nothing lined up. No clients in the pipeline, no events on the books, and no backup plan to pay my bills. But I chose to trust the process. I leaned in with my entire being.

Within three days, I was feeling much better physically, energetically, and I felt more optimistic. I began mentally shifting into gratitude and expectancy, knowing the Universe would bring me opportunities to manifest abundance. On the fourth day, I got a text from a previous client asking if she could pitch my services to her company because she felt my coaching would be a great fit for her entire team.

By the end of that week, we had signed a contract, and the largest invoice of my career was paid. In just a few days, I went from having no idea how I'd cover that month's bills to the biggest deposit my bank account had ever seen.

When I say these tools can change your life, I'm not exaggerating.

That is far from the only example; it's something that's happened more times than I'd ever be able to count. Like I said, when I am focused, I can manifest quickly in both positive and negative ways. And believe me, if you decide to take these tools seriously and get focused, you'll start manifesting much faster than you ever imagined!

You never know how or when your miracle will show up, but it's coming.

Most of the time in life, we feel helpless to change our situations, whatever they may be. But you're not helpless. You can always *choose* to change your perspective and thoughts about any topic. What do you have to lose? Why not give it a try? You have so much to gain.

I've worked with hundreds of clients who've experienced truly incredible results manifesting abundance using their Power Mottos. From unexpected pay raises and bonuses to new job offers with higher pay, to unexpected checks from surprising sources, to business expansion, to unexpected credits or refunds, the list goes on.

Client Example: My client Amanda, who I've had the privilege of working with for several years, used the tools I teach in *Think It* to go from a sales rep at telecom company to an executive vice president in just under five years, quadrupling her income. We used Power Mottos and I AM Statements not only to lay out a new financial future for her but to build her confidence, remove imposter syndrome, and create the version of herself she wanted to become. It's been incredible to watch her transformation over just a few short years.

Imagine how your life might look if your career and income advanced that dramatically in such a short period of time. It is absolutely possible.

Client Example: My clients Cameron and Christopher, a married couple, were part of an advanced reading group for this book. They had no prior knowledge of *Think It* but started using the tools right away—especially Power Mottos and Mental Tennis—and ended up landing their first client!

When they began reading the chapters, they were doing everything they could to get their real estate business off the ground. They'd gotten their licenses months earlier but still hadn't signed a client. Despite going to open houses, networking events, and doing all the "right" things, nothing was working, and they were starting to question whether they'd made the right decision by getting into real estate in the first place. Their frustration and the financial pressure began turning into a real struggle.

But after just a few weeks of consistently practicing these tools, they signed their first listing agreement and momentum had shifted in their favor. Their entire energy changed with each passing week as they applied what they learned in this book. It was incredible to see the frustration turn to hope and the doubt turn to anticipation.

That's the power of alignment. When your thoughts and actions are finally on the same page, *that's* when things start going your way.

Personal Work

To create your customized Power Mottos for the stressors in your life, follow this simple process. In the previous chapter, you identified the top five things that regularly stress you out. Now you're going to write one Power Motto for each of them.

Start by pulling out that personal work and reviewing each stressor. You've already identified the fear or belief underlying each and what you'd like to feel or believe instead. Use that insight and the answers to the following questions to craft a Power Motto that directly addresses each stressor.

- What would be the best-case scenario for each stressor?
- What am I grateful for right now in relation to each stressor?
- What's a good power statement that claims this new best-case outcome for each?

As a reminder, here's the four-step process for writing effective Power Mottos.

Step 1: Acknowledge the Thought (what's the stressor?)
Step 2: What's the Best-Case Scenario?
Step 3: Focus on Gratitude
Step 4: Finish with a Power Statement

Use this process:

1. Stressor: ______________________________
2. Best-case: ______________________________
3. Gratitude: ______________________________
4. Power Statement: _________________________

Here's a flushed-out example to help you write your mottos.

1. **Stressor**: *I'm worried that my relationship will fail. I have this fear that no one will truly love me or that my partner will leave me, because other people have left me in the past.*

2. **Best-case**: *That we have a long and happy life together. That my relationship is healthy, gets stronger, is more committed, and grows deeper every day.*
3. **Gratitude**: *I am grateful for the love of my partner, for the life we're building, and for our commitment to each other.*
4. **Power Statement**: *I am loved and worthy of lasting love!*

Sample Power Motto: *My relationship is strong and healthy; we are building a long and happy life together. I am grateful for their ongoing love and commitment. I am worthy and deserving of their love!*

Now that you've learned how to use Power Mottos to rewire your thoughts and align your mindset with your desired outcomes, it's time to take the next step in transforming how you see yourself.

In the next chapter, we'll dive into what we should be focusing on each day to start creating the life we want. We do this through "daydreaming," a simple tool to train our focus away from the mundane stresses and tasks in our daily life and onto creating a new future with exciting, new outcomes.

This is my favorite part! Let's start creating *you 2.0.*

Chapter 9

Tool #6: Daydreaming

How to Use Visualization to Focus on What You Want and Manifest It Quickly

Offense

Let's talk about one of the most underrated tools for rewiring your mindset and creating a life you truly want: daydreaming. Yes, *daydreaming*—the thing you probably got in trouble for back in middle school. Turns out, it was one of your most powerful mindset tools…you just didn't realize it.

Daydreaming is how we train ourselves to naturally go on *offense*. It's how we stop reacting to the life we have and start mentally rehearsing the life we want to create. And just to be clear, when I say this, I'm not implying that you dislike your current life. Or that you're not grateful for what you have. Or that you shouldn't be proud of everything you've already built. I want to make this point very clear:

It's okay to appreciate your current life and still want *more.*

We need to continue growing, evolving, and up-leveling, otherwise we become stagnant. And who wants to live today on repeat for the rest of their life? Not me.

Here's the best part: Daydreaming is so fun! Visualization is one of the simplest ways to shift your thoughts from the negative into positive energy. It's how you begin building your ideal life, filled with exciting future moments and vivid details of how your desires will manifest. This is where your imagination has permission to run wild, creating the biggest and best versions of everything you want.

I call this *creating a movie in your head.* And it's part of the Centrella Method in the step called See It, from my first book *Hustle Believe Receive,* so my clients and readers have been using this process since 2015, with incredible results.

Why is this tool so important? Because if you can't imagine it, then how can you articulate it? If you can't see it in your mind, how will you know it's what you really want? Your mind has the ability to create a vivid, powerful, and multi-dimensional experience before that experience ever takes place. We can live a moment *before* it happens. And by doing so, we call that moment into our reality on an expedited timeline. How fucking cool is that?

You might be wondering, "But what if I'm not a dreamer?" Here's the truth: You are. I know you are. You were born with ability to imagine, visualize, and daydream, just like everyone else. For some people it might come more naturally, but that doesn't mean you can't be just as skilled.

Maybe you don't see the purpose of daydreaming and think it's a stupid waste of time. I'd argue that you're still engaging this mental muscle weather you realize it or not. Here's a perfect example of how critical this skill can be in getting you exactly what you want.

Imagine hiring an architect to design your dream home. If you don't have a clear idea of what you want, you're immediately going to run into problems. To create an accurate rendering, the architect needs you to clearly and specifically articulate your vision. They'll need the basics, like whether it's a one-story or multi-level home, how any bedrooms and bathrooms, and the general layout. But that's just the start. Before he can bring your dream to life, he'll also need to understand the vibe you want to create. What's the overall aesthetic? What design elements are important to you? What kind of energy do you want people to feel when they enter your home? Who do you see in the home on a daily basis, and who's there for special occasions? Imaging the home with this level of detail plays a critical role in what elements are incorporated in the build. A good architect and design team need all this information and more before they can begin drafting a blueprint and bring your dreams to life.

Now can you see how important our ability to create a detailed mental visual is to our realizing that outcome? And I'm sure you were able to imagine that scenario as you read it, maybe you even pictured your own dream home as you subconsciously answered the above questions. This is how I know that you're going to be a great daydreamer!

You might not know this about me, but I'm known for my "Futureboards" and manifesting tools. I've used my method for "vision boarding," called Futureboards, to completely change my life and to help thousands of people manifest their dream lives as well. You can get all those tools in my number-one best-selling book *#Futureboards.* Visualization is something I've been mastering since 2008, when I started my life over with nothing after my husband left. I started practicing daydreaming purely by accident. I had no money, no job, and no way to support myself or my kids. It was a dark time, to say the least.

To help get me through those early dark days, I began daydreaming about a better life as a subconscious way to escape my bleak reality. I started dreaming about what my new life would look like if—and when—things got better. Each time I'd slip into one of these mini mind movies it would automatically start to lift my spirits, my energy level would increase, my optimism about the future started to grow, and my negative thoughts about my current situation would recede. I began imagining all the fun adventures and experiences I'd have with my children. I started dropping into regular fantasies about what it would feel like to be "successful" in my career, envisioning all the exciting ways that success might manifest. I imagined falling in love and being with a partner who loved and adored me. I dreamed of watching my kids play together outside a villa in Tuscany while I watched the sun set in the distance. On and on those daydreams grew, until they were my undisputed happy place. A mental escape I couldn't wait to explore.

Those daydreams began to save me. They lifted me from the darkness of my everyday life in those early months and helped me envision a whole new future for myself and my children.

I trained myself to create these happy mental escapes every time I was stressed about money, my ex, or just overwhelmed by my new life as a struggling single mom. I could feel that when I focused on all the things I didn't like about my life, those things seemed to get bigger, and I'd feel more out of control and upset about my situation. I hated feeling this way. At the time, much of my life felt like it was spiraling out of my control, and daydreaming was one thing I had total control over to make myself feel better and more hopeful for the future.

Never in a million years did I think that, in doing so, I was tangibly creating those very outcomes. But to my utter shock, that's exactly what I'd done.

About eighteen months after the implosion of my life, those daydreams—and my corresponding Futureboard—started coming to life. First, I was able to take my son on vacation to Hawaii. Then, I got a big promotion which allowed us to move into a nice new home. Then, countless things started showing up in my life exactly how they'd appeared in my daydreams. I was blown away.

And it's never stopped.

That's what started all of this. That's how you're even reading this book, because those early wins sent me on a quest to figure out how I'd made those dreams come to life and how I could keep doing it for the rest of my life. Then I started blogging about what I was learning, and here we are: book four, thousands of clients later, seven countries visited with my children, a son who lived his ultimate dream of playing football at the University of Oregon…and the list goes on. My point?

If I could turn my daydreams into my real life, then you can too.

You already daydream. You just might be using your visualization skills to imagine the *worst-case* scenarios instead of the best. Our brain has this crazy ability to turn a thought into a vivid movie with loads of emotional context. This ability works the same for perceived negative outcomes as it does for positive daydreams. Think about that last time you felt stress or anxiety, you were probably imagining something bad happening. As you did that, your mind created visuals that supported those doomsday thoughts, just like my fear-of-flying example earlier where I kept imagining being on the plane that crashed on 9/11. If you're focus is on what you don't want, your mind will build that more, and your body will begin feeling anxious and fearful. Like I said, you *can* daydream. You just need to proactively practice in the positive context.

How to Practice Daydreaming

This tool teaches you how to flip negative visualizing and learn how to master the art of creating what you *do* want through intentional daydreaming.

Step 1: Pick a Focus

Choose one thing you want to experience. A promotion. A dream trip. A healed relationship. A feeling of financial freedom. Whatever it is, make it specific.

Step 2: Paint the Picture

Imagine where you are, what you're wearing, how it smells, what you hear. Who is with you? What are you eating, doing, or experiencing? Get as vivid as you can. If you struggle with visual details, go on Pinterest and type this experience into the search bar, adding the word "photography" at the end. Make sure you include people in your search. For example: "couple being romantic in Paris photography." Play around on Pinterest as much as you can to spark your visual imagination and jumpstart your mental movie.

Step 3: Add Emotion

To attach emotion (the key ingredient in manifesting this daydream), ask yourself a few simple questions to spark the feelings of desire. What would it be like to be those people in that picture? To feel like that? To live a moment like that? Why would it feel amazing? What about it would light you up? This is how you tap into your custom-created dream and engage your personal desire for that outcome. This emotional contest is the magic ingredient in manifesting using these tools. It's the component that sparks desire, and once we want something and align our thoughts with that outcome, we will make it happen or manifest it.

Step 4: Anchor It in Reality

Tie that visualization to a daily moment—while you're brushing your teeth, driving, working out. Use that time to rehearse it over and over until it becomes exciting and familiar. Keep going back to Pinterest to find more pictures of the "movie" as it evolves. Then, use your mottos and I AM Statements to back up your belief that this new vision is possible for you.

Step 5: Make a Futureboard on Pinterest

Go on Pinterest and search for all your dreams, pinning them to your online #futureboad. A tip is to use the search bar to look for the experience you want, including the people, followed by the word "photography." Example: *Woman cooking in dream kitchen with kids' photography.* This will help your daydream come to life in its first physical form, which is incredibly thrilling! Grab my book *#Futureboards* to get all the detailed instructions.

Client Example: Julie, an amazing client of mine, was struggling to believe she could leave her corporate job and build her coaching business. Every time she thought about quitting, her anxiety spiraled. We used this exact tool to imagine what it would be like to work for herself and have the freedom and flexibility she desired but without the financial stress of leaving her secure job.

She began visualizing her future coaching life every day—walking into her beautiful home office, meeting with ideal clients, and seeing a calendar full of paid sessions. In her mind, she was already there: wearing her favorite outfit, creating content, feeling confident and aligned. She pictured herself at networking events, speaking with ease, proud of the life she'd created, one where she owned her time, set her rates, worked from anywhere and had a job she was passionate about.

We took the time to identify what each of those meant to her. What did "working from anywhere" actually look like in her ideal future? Why would that feel better than her current life as a stressed-out employee? What would it mean to have a truly flexible schedule? Would she be able to send her kids off to school in the morning and be home when they got off the bus? How would she feel as a business owner?

A few weeks later, her company announced large-scale layoffs, but with a twist. Employees had the option to resign and receive a generous severance package instead of waiting to see if they'd be laid off. Because of her long tenure, she qualified for several year's severance—she was literally *paid to leave* her corporate job and fund her new business. It was a blessing beyond anything we could've planned for or even thought to ask for.

Sometimes the Universe is just waiting for you to make your wishes known—so it can swoop in and deliver the "how" in a way that's bigger and better than anything you could've imagined.

Why It Works

Here's what's wild—your brain is so elastic that it doesn't know the difference between a real memory and a vivid, emotionally charged daydream or fantasy. When you visualize something in detail—where you are, how it smells, what you're wearing, how you feel—your brain lights up as if you're actually living that moment. It's so powerful that it can create feelings of excitement, anticipation, and hope: three feelings needed to expedite manifesting. And that's not woo-woo; that's neuroscience. MRI scans show that, when it's done with enough focus and clarity, the same neural pathways activate whether you're remembering something that happened or imagining something you haven't yet experienced. (Note: There's a lot of scientific research on visualization if you want to dive deeper into how and why it works ask Google or ChatGPT to pull studies on it.)

When you practice daydreaming consistently, you're literally training your brain to believe that your vision is real life. And you know what happens when you believe a thought to be true....

This is what makes visualization such a powerful mindset tool. You're triggering your reticular activating system (RAS), the part of your brain that filters your focus and starts scanning for anything that aligns with what you've been imagining. That's why things start to show up, why opportunities start to align. You're not making it up; you're mentally rehearsing your future into existence. That's the science behind manifestation.

Power Mottos: Here are some mottos to help your visualization and daydreaming:

- "If I can see it, I can create it. I am actively creating a life I love!"
- "There will come a day when _______." (Fill in your daydream.)
- "I love watching this magic unfold. I can see it in my mind, so I know it's coming in real life! I can't wait for this ______ to happen!" (Fill in your daydream.)

Personal Work ✍

Grab your journal and answer these prompts to help you customize this work to your life.

- What's one area of my life that I want to be different? (Describe exactly how you want it to look and feel).
- If I could have anything in the world I wanted, what would it be?
- Why do I want it?
- How would I feel if I got it tomorrow?
- What's a moment or experience I can start daydreaming about today?
- Where have I always wanted to visit?
- Why do I want to go there?
- What would I do there?
- Who would go with me? (Create the movie).
- What emotions do I want to feel more often?
- What scenes create those feelings? (For example, if you want to feel more love, what makes you feel loved?)

- What are those actions, done by whom?
- How is my ideal future self different than who I am today?

Pro Tip

Go on Pinterest and create your #futureboard that matches the answers to these questions.

Daydreaming is not a silly fantasy; it's a powerful creation tool. It's how you take your power back from fear, negativity, your current reality, a lack mindset, and doubt. It's how you train your thoughts to support the life you want to create. And it's how you stay focused, motivated, and aligned, especially on the hard days.

Let your mind intentionally wonder about moments and experiences that you want to create. Make it beautiful. Make it exciting! And then watch how your thoughts and focus start to bring your daydream to life.

Chapter 10

Tool #7: The Energy Bubble

How to Protect Your Peace and Stop Being Affected by Other People's Energy

Proactive Defense

Most people are living in a world that is a continuous emotional roller coaster, just along for the ride. They scream and close their eyes on the plunging downhill drop, slamming from side to side, lashing out at everyone around them, or trying to cope as best they can until the ride levels off again. On the rare, smooth spots in between the dramatic rise and fall of this ride, they can find some emotional stability, but all the while their body and nervous system are preparing for the next inevitable slow rise and the unavoidable, terrifying fall. That whole time, they are locked into this insane ride with no control over what happens next.

Does this sound like a fun way to live? I gotta be honest, that's my actual nightmare. Not just as a reality (you're not getting me on a roller coaster, sorry, not happening!) but as a metaphor. That is no way to live. But I bet you could relate, right? Because we've all been there, just waiting with our eyes closed for the ride to end, for a smooth patch to come along and even us back out. Here's the thing: There is zero control in living that way.

When you allow your emotions to hijack your day and send you on a raging coaster of highs and lows, you are giving all your power away. You're essentially strapped into the ride, just waiting for it to end.

But what if you didn't get on the ride in the first place? Everyone around you was pushing you into line and peer-pressuring you to join the insanity. What if you could get out of line and walk away—feeling calm and empowered—and then spend your time doing something you love at the state fair, like watching bunnies? Let's teach our nervous system and our brain how to just watch bunnies for a peaceful goddamn minute and skip the madness. You feel me?

Most of us have gotten so used to reacting to everything around us that we think our emotional state is outside of our control. But emotions are not random; they follow thoughts. And since you've been learning how to train your thinking, you already have the tools to change how you feel in real time, no matter what life throws at you.

Why Emotional Control Matters

The biggest thing people struggle with is regulating how they feel in a moment when they're triggered by a comment, a tone, a look, a text, an action—and that one moment destroys their mood for the rest of the day (or longer).

What is your emotional set point? Everyone has an emotional baseline they return to, often without realizing it. For some people, it's worry, frustration, or stress. For others, it's anger or overwhelm. You might wake up calm, but by mid-morning you've already been pulled into everyone else's energy, and now you're reacting to things that have nothing to do with you. Or you wake up calm, but because you're subconsciously recycling 90 percent of your seventy thousand daily thoughts, you find yourself feeling exactly how you felt yesterday.

Which is hella frustrating because most of us just want to feel good. Am I right? Like, is that too much to ask?

But this is why we sometimes wake up feeling shitty, because we were never taught how to release the thoughts that caused yesterday's feelings of stress, anxiety, worry, anger, frustration, and overwhelm. We didn't know how to train ourselves to consistently feel good, be happy, or feel emotionally regulated. But now we do!

Your emotional set point is shaped by your thoughts, beliefs, and the stories you repeat to yourself. If you've lived in emotional chaos for a long time, then peace will feel unfamiliar. But that doesn't mean it's not available to you. The more you use the *Think It* tools, the more your default set point starts to shift. Over time, your emotional baseline becomes calmer, more grounded, happier, and easier to return to when things feel off. Why? Because every tool in *Think It* teaches you how to intentionally focus on the outcome you want, thereby bringing it into your life.

How to Get in the Energy Bubble

The "Energy Bubble" is a proactive tool to protect your energy *before* you engage with someone who normally triggers you, drains your energy, or is just plain negative or annoying. Think of it like an invisible force field of protection around your mental and emotional space. It helps you hold onto the thoughts and emotions that serve you and reject everything else.

Step 1: Visualize Your Bubble

Take four deep breaths and imagine that you're standing inside a giant clear plastic bubble, like the graphic above (Google Zorbing for more visual inspiration). There's plenty of space to move around and feel safe, do a little yoga, and get a little Zen. There's a layer of plastic protection so strong that you can ram into things and feel no impact at all. Inside the bubble is everything you've been building through this work—your healing, your growth, your energy, your peace. It's filled with all your I AM Statements, Power Mottos, and the new story you're telling yourself daily. Inside this bubble, you are the version of yourself you've always wanted to be. You are actively transforming by doing your offensive work, and in here it surrounds you.

In your bubble you are strong. You are confident. You are smart. Here you are protected, and *you* define you.

Step 2: Protect Your Bubble

Visualize your bubble being protected from the inside out with a coating so thick that negativity and the negative options of others cannot penetrate.

I have faith that you've been diligently completing your Personal Work after each chapter and actively applying the lessons you're learning, so I know you want to protect that hard work. That takes a lot of effort, and I want to commend you for your dedication. All of that hard work is the oxygen you breath in your bubble.

Because of this effort, your energy has begun to shift to a more positive place, and momentum has started building in your favor, so you're naturally gonna be protective of it, right? You wouldn't just let someone walk up to it with a steak knife and pop your bubble. Hell no. This is your protective space, your hard-earned, calm, confident energy.

Step 3: Emotionally Detach from Triggers

Now imagine someone throws a passive-aggressive comment your way or says something rude to you, something that would normally set you off. In the protection of this bubble, you can see it coming, take a deep breath, and get into a mental lotus pose. And instead of that insult cutting like a meat cleaver, it suddenly turns into words written on a piece of paper. You can now decide that those words no longer have the ability to trigger you or the strength to cut through your protective bubble, so they drift on by. They don't even have the stickiness to adhere to the outside of your bubble or penetrate it. You can see them, but you are completely emotionally unphased. They mean nothing to you.

You're busy doing a few downward dogs, a few cobra poses, and maybe a warrior two if you're feeling extra powerful...nothing they can say can disturb your vibe. You are unbothered. They don't define you like they used to, because now *you* define you. They no longer have the power to trigger you, because you're not taking the bait. In fact, the longer you practice this tool the more you can see and hear those words with little or no emotional attachment at all.

Imagine how powerful this makes you. It's insane. I know this tool seems simplistic, but trust and believe it works. And when it works for you, you'll feel superhuman.

What if that annoying coworker no longer had the ability to push your buttons? Now you can hear her/him and see them, but you're not absorbing any of that negative energy or internalizing those comments or actions.

Because you've stopped being a sponge to everything and everyone around you; you're titanium, baby! Just visualize yourself in lotus position, Zen as fuck.

You decide what you let inside your Energy Bubble and what you decline.

When you read that triggering email from your boss, see the text from a family member that sounds awfully accusatory, or hear a negative comment from your partner, ask yourself: *Do I want to receive this? Do I agree with it? Is whatever they just said…really me?* If the answer is *no*, then decline it. Let it fall off your bubble and float away. Say to yourself, *I don't receive that. That is not who I am. I can hear what the other person is saying, but I am choosing not to accept it as my truth.* You're immediately redirecting that internal dialogue.

It's not that you're ignoring what people have to say or that you're not open to constructive feedback, because you are, right? What you are not open to is toxicity, unconstructive "feedback," labels being assigned to you by someone else, negativity that is not yours, or other people's definitions of you. You unsubscribe from all of that.

You can now see all of those things outside your Energy Bubble and choose not to absorb them or make them part of your story. You are now seeing them without emotional connection, just for what they are: someone's opinion, which they are entitled to have.

No one has the power to affect your energy or ruin your day, unless you let them. Remember that! I want you to write that statement down in a place where you'll see it every day—especially if you're regularly dealing with someone at work or a family member who normally triggers you.

Say it out loud. Say it often. Make it your mantra. It will begin working its magic, removing the emotional trigger from those interactions, which will start changing the energy between you and that person for the better.

The Energy Bubble gives you so much power. It teaches you to decide what you allow in and what you don't. You don't need to engage or go into defensive or confrontational mode. You don't need to absorb. You just need to pause, say that motto, and choose to protect your hard-earned positive energy by staying in your bubble.

You are not at the mercy of how other people act or what they say. You get to decide how you feel at any given time.

But not *all the time.* No one can, and that's not our goal. We're not trying to be robots here. We're just trying to gain control in the moments when we'd normally spin into an unhealthy, negative, or even toxic spiral. Those are the ones we want to stop and change. Now that you have these tools, you will always know that you have a choice. You can either choose to ride the coaster like before, or you'll choose to create new, healthier outcomes.

Listen, there are some days when life throws a side punch so hard and so fast that all you wanna do is sit on the floor and have a raging toddler-sized fit (or maybe that's just me). But

I definitely have those days where I just wanna sit down and cry. And when I do, I let all those emotions wash over me—I don't try to suppress them—I feel them all. I allow myself to feel frustrated, upset, tired, overwhelmed, sad, or whatever else. But I also actively try to use my tools to make sure I'm not taking those emotions out on anyone in my life, not my kids, my man, or my friends. I allow venting when it needs to happen, to someone I trust who will hear me without judgment, but also not encourage me to stay stuck in that energy.

When I'm having one of those emotionally charged days, I give myself grace to do whatever I need to do to feel *the feels*. I might eat that pint of ice cream or binge an entire season of *The White Lotus* (again). Whatever I need in that moment, I give it to myself without judgment or guilt.

But that day has a hard deadline, which expires when I go to bed. Meaning, when I wake up, I force myself to start using my tools again to get out of that negative mental state. Having a hard rule of "feel it all for twenty-four hours" holds me accountable to not wallow in that energy. Because I know that the longer I let those emotions go unchecked, the more damage they can do—not only popping my Energy Bubble but also potentially starting to manifest negative outcomes, which I *definitely* don't want.

Note that this is my rule for all the normal stuff life can hurl at you, not the unexpected tragedies or the really big things. I'm not suggesting you can move through those in any set time frame. But for the normal roller coaster stuff, that time limit helps me get to the other side quicker, so I don't get stuck in a funk.

Quick Practices for Emotional Reset

Here are a few tools you can use to regulate your emotional state in real time when you're about to interact with someone who typically triggers you.

Breathe: Close your eyes and take three deep breaths. While you do that, repeat your Power Mottos and I AM Statements that remind you who you are, how you deserve to be treated, and how you want to behave.

Get in Your Energy Bubble: See yourself inside it, protected by all the words you've been telling yourself when you use your offensive tools. See yourself as the embodiment of those positive statements. Remind yourself that you have changed, that you show up differently now, that no one has the power to trigger you unless you let them. Tell yourself you are proud of how well you're handling the situation.

Excuse Yourself: Walk out of the room if possible. Take a second to give yourself a minute to breathe.

Talk Yourself Through It: Go into a bathroom if you can and look at yourself in the mirror. Tell yourself who you are (your I AM Statements) and how you want to feel, be, and act in that moment (your Power Mottos). If you can, say them out loud to yourself in the mirror; if not, say them in your head in any moment or any situation.

Personal Work

Grab your journal and answer these questions to help you identify and disarm your emotional triggers.

- Who or what tends to hijack my emotional state?

- What do they normally do or say that triggers me? (List some of these behaviors, actions, or words so you can see how those things have affected you).
- What normally happens when I'm upset or emotionally triggered by this person or situation? How do I normally respond or act?
- Why do I react this way? Can I think of healthier ways to respond or deal with these situations?
- What is my normal emotional set point, and what do I want it to be?
- What old emotional patterns or reactions do I want to change?
- How does my body, mind, and energy feelwhen it's protected and calm?
- What helps me feel regulated and emotionally in control?

Pro Tip 1

Try assuming positive intent. Ask questions rather than assume. Seek to understand the other person rather than assume their intentions. It's easy to jump to conclusions or assume the worst when you already have weird energy or bad blood with a person. But can you take a quick step back to objectively ask yourself, are you assuming ill intent? If so, maybe try assuming positive intent. Maybe they didn't intentionally try to hurt you or even realize they have. Have you ever verbalized your feelings to them? Not everyone is self-aware enough to know when they are being rude, mean, condescending, hurting your feelings, or behaving badly. So maybe it's time to tell them?

Pro Tip 2

If you have a toxic or triggering person in your life that you have to frequently interact with, change their photo in your phone to your Energy Bubble. You can go on Canva and make your own custom bubble, just like I did for the graphics in this chapter. Just pick a bubble and then search for a man or woman doing something you enjoy or something that reminds you to stay calm and put them in the bubble, then save as an image, and voilà!

In part 3, I'll show you how to apply the *Think It* tools to real-life situations and the areas most people want to improve across every aspect of life.

Part Three

Think It in Action

How to Apply the Tools in Real Life

Living It

Now that you've learned the foundational concepts and mastered the seven core *Think It* tools, it's time to apply them to your actual everyday life. This is where the work gets real, because knowing the tools is one thing, but *using* them in the moments that matter is what transforms your mindset, your confidence, and your outcomes.

In this section, I'll walk you through how to use each tool in response to some of the most common real-life questions I've heard over the years from my coaching clients, readers, and audience. These are the challenges that keep people stuck, frustrated, and overwhelmed.

Questions like: "How do I stop spiraling when I get anxious?" "How do I stop caring so much about what other people think?" "What do I do when I doubt myself and feel like a fraud?" "How do I rebuild confidence after failure?" "What's the first step when I don't know what I want anymore?"

Each chapter in this section is focused on one of those real-life moments. I'll share a relatable example, break it down using the tools you've learned, and walk you through exactly how to apply them step-by-step, so you're not just reading mindset theory, you're practicing it in the places it matters most. These are the conversations I've had in one-on-one coaching sessions, in social media DMs, on stage, and with myself on the hardest days of my own journey.

Because mindset training isn't about being perfect or positive all the time. It's about learning to use your tools *in the moment*, when the fear hits, when the overthinking kicks in, when you want to say no to something you actually want, or when someone's words threaten to unravel your progress. These are the moments that shape your life. And now, you'll know exactly what to do when they come.

You'll also see how the tools can be layered together. Maybe you'll use the Power of Pause and Mental Tennis to stop a negative spiral, then reinforce that shift with your Power Mottos and I AM Statements. Or you'll combine daydreaming and identity work to start showing up as the future version of you.

This section is designed to build your confidence, show you the power of your tools in action, and help you start thinking like the person you're becoming. You're ready to use your mind as the most powerful asset you have. Let's get into it.

Growth Mindset

Build Self-Confidence, Overcome Imposter Syndrome, and Silence Your Inner Critic

Chapter 11

How Do I Get More Confident and Stop Feeling Like a Fraud?

How to Ditch Imposter Syndrome for Good

IRL Example: You get offered a big opportunity…and immediately want to say no. Let's say you've been quietly dreaming about something—a leadership role, a speaking gig, or an opportunity to share your voice or start a business. And then… it happens. You're asked to take the lead on a big project, someone invites you to be a guest on a podcast, or you get asked to submit your work for an award. Your gut reaction should be excitement, right?

But instead, panic sets in. That little voice creeps in: *Who do you think you are? You're not ready. Someone else would be better for this.*

You feel that tightness in your chest, the urge to shrink. You start looking for a way to politely decline or pass the opportunity to someone "more qualified." Sound familiar? That's not your truth talking. That's some of your old blocks and beliefs surfacing.

First, you want to ask yourself a few simple questions to see if this is your manifestation waiting to be received. Remember all those new outcomes we've been speaking into existence using Mental Tennis, I AM Statements, and Power Mottos? They will start to manifest, which is incredibly exciting! But…

Most people miss their manifestations because they don't know how to *receive* the thing they've asked for. Why? Because it usually comes through the back door, a side entrance, or it shows up in an unrecognizable package, so you've gotta be ready to recognize it through the disguise of "real life."

Those new outcomes you've been defining and daydreaming about will start showing up in one of two ways….

1. **As an Opportunity**: Like someone asking you to speak, lead a project, submit your name for a promotion, or any number of ways opportunities can show up.
2. **As an Idea**: You know when you suddenly get an inspired idea while running on the treadmill (that's literally how I got the idea and steps for my first book, *Hustle Believe Receive*), walking the dog, or sitting in traffic?

Ask yourself: *Did I ever ask for any part of this?*

Take a moment to really think about it, examine the idea or opportunity from every angle. It might not look the way you expected the "how" to show up, but could it lead to something you've wanted or asked for? Is it a step in that direction? Could it be part of the journey, and is your job, at this moment, to simply trust the process?

Then ask yourself: *When I think about doing this thing or taking this opportunity, how do I feel?* Here, you're looking for a mix of excitement at the possibilities it represents and a little fear, which is totally normal. But what you really want to pay attention to is this: *When I flesh out all the potential positive outcomes, does it line up with what I know I want? Does it get me excited?* If so, it's your manifestation.

And lastly, you want to ask yourself: *Is the reason I want to say no—or "not right now"—coming from a place of lack or fear?* If it is, then you absolutely *must* take it.

Because you never want your decisions to come from lack or fear—those are blocks. And they might just be trying to keep you from receiving the very thing you've been waiting for.

Now that we know how to vet an opportunity, we want to use our *Think It* tools to act on this manifestation.

Mental Tennis: You immediately want to start reversing the negative and limiting inner dialogue that was your first gut reaction. Do this by running the full sequence:

See It: *Why am I automatically rejecting this idea or opportunity?*
Stop It: *Wait a second, I'm no longer acting out of fear. What do I want instead?*
Replace It: *I am ready for this opportunity. I am excited by this possibility. I can learn as I go. I'm ready for this!*

You want to actively reverse any of those negative and self-defeating thoughts and beliefs and replace them with how you *want* to feel and how you *want* to show up, so you can immediately begin building your confidence instead of tearing it down.

Talk Yourself Through It: Implant the internal dialogue that supports your dreams, builds you up, and helps you have the strength and confidence to say yes. *This is something I've wanted, and I'm scared because it's new. That's not a reason to walk away; it's a reason to lean in. Of course I don't feel "ready." No one does the first time. That doesn't mean I'm not capable. I've done something new before. This is no different.*

Look for the Positive What-Ifs: What if this turns out better than you expected? What would that mean for your long-term goals, dreams, and career? What if it leads to other opportunities and is the stepping stone you've waited for? What if it's a huge success?

Power Mottos: Start reinforcing the new belief loop with fresh Power Mottos and I AM Statements that help get you ready. Write out your own or use any of these that resonate and say them out loud:

- "I was made for this!"
- "I am ready to be seen!"
- "I'm becoming more confident every day."
- "I am proud of myself for stepping up!"
- "I trust myself to make good decisions."
- "I am capable. I am ready."
- "I am excited for what's to come."
- "I belong here. I bring value."
- "My voice and talents are needed and appreciated."

Every time the doubt creeps in, go back to these. Let them do their magic.

Daydream: Close your eyes. Visualize the version of you who already feels confident. What are you wearing? Picture yourself in that power outfit. How do you walk into a room?

How do you respond to praise, to pressure, to being seen? How do people react to you, and how do they treat you?

Confidence doesn't mean being the loudest or "smartest" person in the room. It's not about knowing everything or being cocky. It's not about constant external validation.

Confidence is about genuinely knowing your strengths and leading with them. It's about believing in your ability to handle new and challenging situations—and knowing that you will continue to improve.

Take the Opportunity! Don't wait until you "feel ready" because you never will. Especially if it's a great opportunity, it should be outside your comfort zone. You'll question your qualifications, your timing, your ability—but so would anyone standing in your shoes for the first time. That fear isn't a warning; it's an invitation. It's what comes with dreaming big and pushing yourself to achieve your next level of success.

Say yes. Show up scared but eager to learn, with an inquisitive mind, not a "fronting" attitude. You're learning. That's expected. That's how confidence is built—through action, through repetition, through proof, and through keeping your word to yourself.

You become confident by doing the thing. Not by waiting to feel ready.

And let me just say one last thing:

You don't have imposter syndrome.

Stop labeling yourself with it; that alone holds you back. This term enables you to justify passing on your potential, your dreams, and your manifestations. Stop!

It's simply *learning*. That's all it is. Every time you ever did something for the first time, you felt unqualified, like you were faking it, like someone would wake up and realize you actually didn't belong—that's part of the normal process of stretching past your comfort zone. But what happened in all those past jobs, positions, or things you tried? If you kept at it, you got better, you knew more, and you learned. So, just be willing to learn and be open about the fact that you are. As you gain knowledge and expertise, use your Power Mottos to reinforce your new story about your capabilities.

And that, my friend, is how you go from someone who was afraid to act because you felt riddled with self-doubt to a confident genuine expert at doing the thing.

Do the thing.

Chapter 12

Why Do I Always Compare Myself to Others and Feel Like I'm Not Good Enough?

How to Silence Your Inner Critic

We all have that ugly inner critic. I call mine "the nasty bitch." She's the devil on my shoulder, trying to take me back to old patterns, beliefs, and behaviors. For most of us, that voice has been with us so long that we think it's just who we are. But it's not. It's just a conglomerate of voices we've heard throughout our life—from society, family, friends, teachers, classmates, bosses, coworkers, and, of course, our own self-judgments. It's one big nasty cauldron, a witch's brew of self-defacing, critical, ugly thoughts—not *truths*, just repetitive thinking. It's so ingrained that sometimes it's hard to tell the truth from a self-taught lie.

You, like most of us, have been collecting evidence to support the belief that you're not ready, not good enough, or that others are somehow more qualified. Over time, that pattern turned into a story you started to accept as truth. But it's not truth—it's just a narrative you've been unconsciously reinforcing. You've been using the very concepts in this book to strengthen limiting beliefs—just in the wrong direction. And if you could do that without even realizing it, imagine what's possible when you start doing it on purpose, in the direction of what you actually want.

Many of us grew up learning to criticize ourselves before anyone else could. It became our armor. I know it was mine. Having always struggled with my weight, I used to mention it ad nauseam to everyone in a self-deprecating, "funny" way, hoping that if I brought it up, people would know I knew and therefore judge me less. Such warped thinking! But it was my reality before I learned these tools, so I get it.

Mental Tennis: The second that voice pops up with its doubt, judgment, or shame, hit the thought back. You know the drill:

See It: *I'm thinking that other people are better than me and that I'm not good enough.*

Stop It: *I'm no longer being self-critical. It never served me in the past, and I'm done with it! I won't let old beliefs sabotage my progress.*

Replace It: *I am enough. I am ready! I will learn as I go. I'm not comparing myself to anyone any more.*

This is your moment to separate your identity from your old programming. Just because it feels familiar doesn't mean it's true. Challenge it every time, replacing it with how you want to feel instead.

Power Mottos: Use these to rewire that inner dialogue. Say them in the mirror. Say them before you walk into the meeting. Say them every time doubt tries to creep in:

- "I trust myself."
- "I have nothing to prove."
- "I am more than enough right now."
- "I'm proud of how far I've come."
- "I'm learning, growing, and doing the work."
- "I compare myself to no one."
- "The person I seek validation from is myself. Being proud of me is what matters."
- "I am capable and confident."
- "I am daily transforming into the person I wanna be."

Personal Work

Grab your journal and answer the following prompts to help you customize this work for you.

- What are the most common things my inner critic tells me?
- Where do I think those thoughts originally came from?
- Whose voice does it sound like?
- What are three reasons that voice is wrong?
- What do I want to believe instead?
- What does the confident version of me sound like?
- What do I want to believe about myself and my capabilities?
- How do I want to feel on a daily basis?

This is how you do the work. This is how you build real confidence: by not trying to ignore the critic but by changing it all together.

Chapter 13

How Do I Stop Internalizing Criticism?

How to Stop Second-Guessing Yourself

IRL Example: Family criticism triggers guilt or shame. You're excited about a great job you just got—with the biggest salary you've ever made—and you tell a family member who says something like, "Oh, you're big time now! I guess you don't need us little people anymore."

Suddenly, you feel chastised, guilty, and start questioning yourself, wanting to diminish your achievement and apologize for your success.

Here's how to apply the tools:

The Energy Bubble: Close your eyes and get in your cozy protective bubble, filled with all those beautiful positive I AM Statements and Power Mottos you've been telling yourself. Take a deep breath. Let it bounce off your bubble. Smile and say, "Now, you know that's not who I am. I'm excited to start the job. It's a new chapter, one I've worked really hard for." Then say, "Can I grab you something to drink? I'm gonna go grab a drink." And just exit the convo.

You are rejecting their negativity in a way that doesn't cause further confrontation and validates your accomplishment for *yourself*, showing them that they crossed a boundary and that the comment didn't hit its intended target.

Talk Yourself Through It: Say something like, *That is just how they are. I'm not going to let it bother me or ruin my night. I have worked hard to get where I am, and I'm proud of myself for getting this job and making more money. I refuse to let them make me feel guilty! This does not make me selfish. It does not mean I'll abandon my family. I do not think I'm better than anyone. I refuse to accept that negative energy. I chose not to let this affect me; it's not who I am.*

Power Mottos: "I decide who I am, and I'm proud of who I am. I make good decisions and trust my intuition."

You get to define who you are—not them.

So, remind yourself of that in those moments and let comments like that bounce off your bubble, because they can't stick. They can't get to you if you know who you are. Nothing they can say can shake you, because in that moment, you have the tools to instantly rewrite that internal dialogue and reaffirm who you are and who you want to be. No one has the power to take that away from you unless you give it to them.

Chapter 14

How Do I Stop Caring About What Other People Think?

How to Protect Yourself from the Judgment of Others

You may have heard that when women hit their forties, they enter an era of "no fucks to give." It's true. I swear, the second I turned forty, it was like a switch flipped—and as hard as I looked, I couldn't find a single fuck to give: not about what people thought about me or what they said about me. That whole line of "Are they judging me?" thinking just vanished. I wish it had happened thirty years earlier.

Since then, I've talked to so many women who've experienced something similar. But if you haven't hit that liberating shift yet, here's the good news: You don't have to wait. You can *train* yourself to stop caring what other people think and start building a belief system that makes you feel safe, grounded, and confident in who you are—at any age, in any room.

This is how you can proactively train yourself to not give a fuck what people say—at *any* age. It's how you start detaching from the emotional drama you create when you try to assume what people are thinking or saying about you.

Because honestly...*who cares?*

Seriously—who are you so worried about impressing? Whose imaginary opinion is running your inner world right now? Why do you waste so much of your precious energy obsessing over what other people might think of you?

Like so many women, I spent way too much of my life performing for an invisible audience. I wondered: *Am I good enough? Do they like me? Do they think I belong here?* It took me years to realize that none of it matters—not the perceived judgment, not the silence, not the snide remarks or backhanded compliments. Their opinions don't define your worth, your success, or your future. They never did. But here's the truth most of us don't figure out until later: The only opinion that really matters is your own. The sooner you learn that, the sooner you're free.

Most people are too busy thinking about themselves to be thinking about you.

I know that stings a little—but it's honestly the most freeing realization you can have. People aren't obsessing over you. They're obsessing over *themselves*—over their own lives, their own insecurities, and yes, often about *what you think of them.* That means all the energy you're spending on imaginary judgment? It's just wasted fuel.

You get one life. Your opinion is the one that matters most. You're the only one who has to live your life. You're the one who wakes up in your body, hears your thoughts, and faces your challenges. So why are you giving other people's opinions more weight than your own? The most important relationship you'll ever have is with yourself—so let's start treating it like that.

Once you really internalize those two truths, everything shifts. You stop shape-shifting. You stop shrinking. You stop explaining. You start showing up for yourself in a whole new way. And *that's* when confidence is born. Not from praise. Not from perfection. And definitely not from waiting until you "feel ready." Confidence is something we *build*—choice by choice, thought by thought, tool by tool.

So, what do you do when someone *does* throw judgment your way?

Remind yourself that no one has the power to define you *but you*.

Use these tools. Anytime someone tries to label you, throw a passive-aggressive comment your way, or try to trigger old shame stories—call it out for what it is. You can calmly refute their accusation in a way that doesn't make them defensive and doesn't create a bigger issue (if you don't want one). Say something simple and direct like, "Now that's not fair to say—I don't appreciate that." This helps them realize that they've hit your boundary. Then, affirm for *yourself* who you are.

Mental Tennis: Practice Example

See It: *I'm thinking that people are judging me*
Stop It: *I'm no longer worried about what other people think.*
Replace It: *I know who I am and no one can define me, but me. I'm not giving my power away anymore!*

Continue to reverse any negative thoughts to prevent a spiral and fill that space with your I AM Statements to redefine yourself.

Chapter 15

Building Confidence Q&A

Here are some of the most common questions I get asked about how to build genuine confidence and the advice I give my clients.

How Do I Build Confidence When I've Never Had It?

My guess is that you *have* felt confident about something at some point in your life. You might not consider yourself a self-confident person, but that doesn't mean you haven't been confident in certain situations, environments, or circumstances.

Think back through your life—was there a time when you did something and felt good about it? Maybe you received praise and encouragement and, as a result, felt like you could do that thing again? Do you have a driver's license? Have you ever had a first day of work? Do you know how to ride a bike? Get my drift?

There are things in your life that you are so confident about that you take them entirely for granted. But the truth is, when you first learned to drive a car, you were probably terrified and not at all confident in your ability to drive. You probably thought everyone else was better at it than you were—and you were right. They had more practice and experience. But what happened? As you kept driving and pushed yourself to drive on the freeway, on country roads, at night, and alone—your confidence began to grow.

I know this firsthand because over the past seven years, I've taught my three kids to drive. I started with each one when they were fifteen—I made them get permits and put them behind the wheel. I had them drive in all kinds of weather and conditions, and none of my kids wanted to do it. (Which, by the way, don't get me started on this generation of kids who don't want to learn to drive! At sixteen, I couldn't wait to get my license and be off on my own—but I digress.)

My kids did not want to learn to drive, but I did not give them that option. To me, driving is a necessary life skill—especially for young women—so no, I wasn't about to let them off the hook.

I realized very quickly as I began to teach them (yes, I taught them exclusively myself) that I needed to provide them with positive affirmation during the entire process to build their confidence. I minimized the mistakes that were minimal and pointed out the bigger errors without tearing them down or scaring them. I strangely had a total body calm when I was teaching them—probably because I sensed that was what they needed: to not fear the road or the car, but conquer it and build their belief that they could drive safely in all situations.

I gave them all their own mottos and affirmations and would say them out loud as they walked out the door to drive alone once they had their license. They needed to know how to talk to themselves so that confidence would grow. And it did. I'm happy to report that they are all safe, confident, and very capable drivers.

And I bet you are too. You went through that process as well. So if you could do it then, you can do it now. If you can be confident in one area of life, you can rinse and repeat that process to be confident at anything.

Confidence is created by doing these two things: controlling what you tell yourself and getting practice at doing the thing. That's it.

You cannot gain confidence just by doing step one. You can tell yourself all day long how capable you are, but if you never put it to the test—if you never actually do the thing—that belief will not stick.

You can, however, become confident over time just by doing the thing. That is called "fake it till you make it," and I've mastered that skill all my life, long before I ever knew how to control my inner dialogue. So if you're one of those people—who, like me, can figure it out as you go and have, over time, built up enough trust in yourself that things will generally work out—then confidence can turn from "fake" to real with enough practice.

But if that's not you and faking it triggers your feelings of being an "imposter," then you have to align your inner dialogue with the action you take. Plus, doing this will result in building genuine confidence ten times faster than by only doing the thing—and we all want faster results!

So, the answer is...you have built confidence in the past and you can do it again using your I AM Statements, Mental Tennis, and Power Mottos...and by doing the thing!

How Do I Stop Shrinking in Rooms Where I Feel Less Experienced or Qualified?

I know this all too well. See, I taught myself to read when I was thirteen years old. I had no formal education until my freshman year of high school and did not graduate from college. So this is something I struggled with for a long time. Everyone in a given room was "smarter" than me—because pretty much everyone I know has a college degree. So, in my head, that automatically made them smarter. My whole life, I've been the only person I've ever met who grew up homeless and uneducated, so in my head, everyone was also much better than me in every way.

But early in my life, I learned that since I could not change these facts, I could get wise—I could observe, adapt, and apply what I saw to become street smart. That has served me well, I can't lie. It helped me adapt in any room or situation so that I didn't stick out like a sore thumb. It helped me assimilate. But it wasn't until I learned what my core strengths were that I gained genuine confidence to speak up and lend my voice anywhere, including rooms with powerful and influential people. I owned my weaknesses and didn't try to mask them, but I also leaned into my strengths and led with those. This allowed me to garner the respect and attention of powerful people—ones who previously would have intimidated the shit out of me.

It is so important to know your strengths and lead with them.

What are you good at? Listening to people? Understanding them? Asking insightful questions? Providing honest and real feedback? Being a good friend? Being a critical thinker? Your attention to detail? Your loyalty or trustworthiness? What are your natural gifts? I know you have several so think about your personality traits, your character, and other intangibles. If you really don't know, ask the people in your life who you trust. Just say, "Hey, I'd love your feedback. What's something you think about when you think of me? Something that defines me for you? Or something you think I do well?" It's always interesting to see how other people view us—and I bet they will share things you never even thought of.

I realized that some of my natural gifts are building meaningful relationships with just about anyone I come in contact with. I have a unique ability to read people and make them feel seen, heard, and understood on a deeper level—almost immediately. I have a skill for asking thoughtful, deep questions because I'm genuinely curious, and this helps people open up and feel safe. I was in my mid-to-late thirties when I realized these were strengths, and it took a while to learn how to lead with them, but now I can honestly say they are what make me an exceptional coach. I don't say that to be cocky—I say that from genuine experience and confidence that has been built over time by coaching thousands of people and watching their lives transform.

The short answer is this: Stop comparing yourself to everyone else in the room. There is only one you in the entire world—let alone in any room—so what you bring is incredibly unique and valuable. No one, no matter how hard they try, can replicate that. It's your superpower.

Wear your uniqueness, your story, your history, and your talents with pride. Let them lead with quiet graceful confidence. They are, after all, the things you know best about yourself—so don't try to copy someone else's superpower. Focus on how you hone your own.

How Can I Believe in Myself When I've Failed Before?

There is no such thing as failure. And that's coming from someone who's "failed" more times than I can count. I've had everything and lost it all multiple times. I've started businesses that I've had to close. I've bought a house and lost it in foreclosure. I've released a book that no one ever saw or read. I've been fired from a job. I've spent years in multiple colleges but never graduated. So…yeah, a lot of people would call that failure.

But I don't. Because every single one of those things taught me valuable lessons that helped me to be more successful in the long run or at the next thing I tried. Those setbacks aren't fun; that's true. I never loved going through them, but they happened for a reason, and they molded me into the odd little anomaly that I am today. Those "failures" also lit massive fires under my motivation, which has fueled my success.

Because though I've had a book "fail," I've also gotten four book deals when no one but me believed I could get one! Losing the house helped me shift my priorities to what kind of life I wanted to live and what type of childhood I wanted to provide for my children. So instead of buying another one, I took my kids to seven countries throughout their upbringing. Being fired from that job is what gave me the push to start my coaching business, which—though not easy—has been the best decision of my life. Closing businesses helped me get clear on what I wanted to focus on and who my ideal client is.

I want you to start rebranding "failure" as "learning." Because that is what it truly is. It's your classroom. It's your hands-on training center. It's the education you must have in order to get to where you ultimately want to go. It's necessary. It's needed. It's the price of success.

If you've never failed at anything, have you really *lived?*

Life is about learning, adapting, pivoting, adjusting, and honing. It's not about getting on a straight freeway to success. No road on the planet is straight forever. Ever been on a road trip that never had a curve, a hill, an accident along the way, a lane closed? No. Life is like that—it's supposed to be composed of *all the things.*

Personal Work

So, the short answer is to get out your journal and ask yourself:

- *What have I learned from my past "failures?"*
- *What will I never do again?*
- *How can I avoid making those same mistakes?*
- *What did I learn that I want to take with me and get better at next time?*
- *Why did that "failure" happen? What were the exact decisions I made that contributed to this? Why did I make them? What would I do differently next time?*

Note: If you think that your past failures were created by external factors or were the fault of other people, circumstances, or anything else—think again.

You were part of that outcome—so ask yourself, *What role did I play?* You've got to get real here. Don't go soft on yourself, because that does you a disservice. Denial is not your friend when you're doing a postmortem on a "failure." If you're not brutally honest with yourself, you'll end up repeating the exact same mistakes and land right back where you started. You have to learn the lesson, or it will keep showing up. And if that failure was painful, use it. Let it fuel you. Be determined to change what's in your control so you can adjust, grow, and use that knowledge to succeed faster next time.

Lastly, this question comes down to fear and self-doubt. To remove both, use your Power Mottos, I AM Statements, and daydreaming tools to identify what success will look like next time—and build the confidence through your tools to get back out there and try again.

Money Mindset

Begin Manifesting More Abundance and Start Growing Wealth

Chapter 16

I Got a Raise but Am Still Living Paycheck to Paycheck, Why Did Nothing Change?

How to Go from Lack to Abundance

IRL Example: You finally get the raise you've been working toward. It's a win. It should feel like relief, but instead your first thoughts are these: *It's still not enough. Everything's just going to cost more now anyway. I should save it in case something bad happens.*

Before the money even hits your account, you're already mentally spending it or hoarding it. And just like that, the scarcity mindset creeps right back in. Sound familiar? I've been there. That old programming takes diligence to rewire, but it *can* be done and when you're consistent, the results will always follow.

Let's break it down using your tools.

Using the Power of Pause: The moment you start spiraling with anxious thoughts about money…

1. Remember to *pause*. Ask yourself: *Is there anything I can do about this right now? No. So worrying about it is only creating more lack, and I refuse to do that.*
2. Ask yourself, what do I want *instead?* Claim that as your new outcome, *I am abundant, money is coming into my life quickly and easily.*
3. Change the subject. Quickly change the topic of thought in your mind to something you want to manifest. Daydream about the day when you get to take your dream trip or what it will feel like to have more than enough money in your bank account. Allow yourself to feel the hope, relief, and anticipation of your financial situation improving. It's the fastest way to manifest more money!

Using Mental Tennis: Start reversing the limiting beliefs that pop up. Play it out like this:

See It: *Why am I focusing on what I don't have instead of being thankful for the abundance I just received?*

Stop It: *I refuse to continue creating lack. I'm switching my mindset to gratitude.*

Replace It: *I'm so thankful for this raise! It is proof that I am manifesting more abundance every day.*

Using Power Mottos: Write five power mottos about money to help change your subconscious beliefs from lack to abundance. Say them proactively every day to preempt and circumvent thoughts of lack, until you believe them with every fiber of your being.

Here are a few examples, but write ones that feel powerful to you as well:

- "I am worthy and excited to receive financial abundance."
- "I deserve and will receive success and prosperity!"
- "Abundance is on its way to me!"
- "Money flows to me easily and often from unexpected sources."
- "I am grateful to provide a beautiful life for myself and my family."
- "I'm ready to receive all forms of abundance."
- "I am making good financial decisions and growing generational wealth."
- "There is always more where that came from!"
- "I love money, and money loves me!"
- "Having money allows me to be a blessing to the people around me. It feels great to pass it on!"

Notice how most of those have an exclamation at the end? That is to encourage you to say them with conviction, excitement, and an exclamation! Believe it or not, this helps you internalize these words even faster and provides you with a shot of empowerment every time you say them with pizazz. This encourages the *feeling* of abundance, which is a powerful manifesting multiplier.

Pro Tip

This is one little thing I do to remind myself that financial abundance is on its way: every time my left palm itches, I take a moment to say, "Ooh la la! Money is on its way!" Then I make sure to give that palm a nice scratch. Legend says that when your left palm itches, it means money and prosperity are on their way. You better believe I'm claiming it every single time!

Instead of brushing past the raise or unexpected income—*celebrate it.* Treat it like proof that your abundance is real. That it's working. That you're growing. Say: "This is evidence that I can and am manifesting more money! I receive it with gratitude."

Every time you acknowledge your progress with gratitude and joy, you expand your capacity to receive more. That's the energy of abundance. Celebrating these wins is huge, and if you don't, it will slow your progress and stop more abundance from coming.

Remember that when you first start manifesting abundance, it comes in packages you'd normally not necessarily associate with a manifestation. It might be something small at first—like someone else picking up a lunch tab when you expected to pay. Or the car in front of you at the Starbucks drive-through unexpectedly paying for your morning coffee (if this has never happened to you, it will—and when it does, pass it on one day). It might be an unexpected coupon or discount for the thing you expected to pay full price for. Add that money up! That is money in your pocket—a.k.a. manifested abundance.

If you shrug it off as nothing, it will stop your momentum. Be grateful! Do a little money dance. Express gratitude.

Client Example: I recently had a client who was working on changing her money beliefs from lack to abundance, and after four weeks of doing this work, she manifested $30,000! But here's the insane part—she didn't even realize or recognize that she'd done this and was about to shrug it off as nothing. As she relayed this information at a coaching session, she nonchalantly mentioned how she'd gotten an unexpected grant for half the tuition to a program she was planning to enroll in. Then she received an unexpected coupon discount for another $5,000 of it, and then her job covered another portion of the program. It totaled $30,000!

I stopped her and said, "Hold up girl. You're telling me that you just manifested this program being paid for, and you're still focusing on *lack*? What is happening here? Do you realize that you just manifested $30,000! Like holy shit!" She paused, and the light went on. "I guess you're right. I hadn't thought about it like that." *How did you think about it?* I wanted to say but held my tongue.

But she is not alone. When people begin manifesting, they almost always miss their manifestations or are not grateful for them. I can hear you thinking, *That would never be me! I'd never miss something like that.* But honestly, you probably would. Because most people are only looking for an unexpected check to come in the mail, which is not how this works, not at first anyway. Think of all the times you got a gift card, someone picked up the tab for something, or you got an unexpected discount at the register when buying that shirt...did you throw a gratitude party and mentally put that saved money back in your bank account and thank the Universe for your abundance deposit? Probably not. But you will from now on, right?

If you can notice and show gratitude for all the blessings you have right now in your life, as is...then the Universe will continue to show up for you.

The more you're grateful for what you have, the more you'll get to be grateful for. And as you get better at this—more grateful and expectant—the undeniable checks will follow in all sorts of ways. Unexpected money will begin coming into your life: whether that's through promotions, new job opportunities, new side hustle ideas, new clients coming into your business, and so on. The ways are endless. But be a good steward of what you have now. Show that you can be present and thankful; that's how you expedite all the good stuff.

Chapter 17

What If Deep Down I Don't Believe I Deserve More, and I Feel Guilty for Even Wanting It?

How to Rewire Guilt and Limiting Beliefs Around Money

IRL Example: You dream about more...and then immediately feel ashamed. You sit down to journal or scroll Pinterest for your Futureboard (my method for manifesting in my second book *#Futureboards*), and you catch yourself daydreaming about things you'd love—more income, financial freedom, travel, a beautiful home, a dream vacation. For a moment, you feel inspired and even a little giddy at all the amazing possibilities the world has to offer.

And then those old nasty thoughts kick in like these: *That's selfish. It's not spiritual to want that much. People with money are greedy. I should be happy with what I already have. People like me don't live like that.*

You shut the tab. Put the pen down. You tell yourself you're being "realistic." But what's actually happening is that you've hit a deeply rooted belief system that says: *I don't deserve more. Wanting more makes me a bad person.*

If that's been your experience, you're not alone. It's something I've seen in so many of my clients over the years, especially those raised in religious or faith-based households. I was raised by extremely religious parents myself, so I know how deeply that early messaging, like "take from the rich and give to the poor," can embed itself. Even long after I stopped identifying with those beliefs, the guilt and shame around success lingered. That kind of programming runs deep, and it can quietly sabotage your ability to feel safe receiving abundance.

Here's what I know for sure: There is more than enough abundance for all of us. The Universe is limitless, and our potential to manifest its riches is also limitless. The limits lie in our beliefs and blocks to receiving it.

I've never been upset after receiving a big check. Signing a new client and getting paid has never once ruined my day. Has it ever pissed you off? Of course not. It brings joy, relief, even excitement. Those aren't selfish or shameful emotions, they're natural. So why should gratitude and happiness around receiving money make you feel guilty? It shouldn't. You're allowed to feel good about receiving abundance, and the more joyful you feel, the more it will continue to manifest.

To those who claim money doesn't buy happiness, I say—then you've likely never gone without it. Because when you have, you know that having money absolutely brings relief, reduces stress, creates freedom, and allows you to give generously. And all of that feels a lot like happiness to me.

If you want to uncover the root of your beliefs around money—whether it's guilt, shame, fear, or lack, you have to be willing to do the inner work. We can't change what we haven't brought to the surface. That's why this journaling exercise is essential, it helps you identify the unconscious patterns that need to shift so you can create a new relationship with money.

What to Do When You Start Feeling Guilty for Wanting More

Those old feelings won't die out overnight, so when they do pop back up, use your *Think It* tools.

Mental Tennis: As always, Mental Tennis is the quickest and easiest way to start reversing our beliefs, and the more you use it the faster and better you'll get at applying it.

See It: *I am feeling bad for wanting more.*
Stop It: *But that is the old me. I've worked hard to release that limiting belief; it no longer serves me.*
Replace It: *I am worthy and deserving of wealth and abundance. I can want more and still be kind, spiritual, and generous. The more I have, the more I can bless others.*

You're not choosing greed. You're choosing expansion. The Universe is not scarce—it's limitless. And there's more than enough for you *and* everyone else, so hit that ball back over the net!

Power Mottos: Here are some examples

- "Abundance allows me to give freely and joyfully."
- "The more I receive, the more I give."
- "Wealth amplifies my purpose."

- "There is enough for everyone."
- "My success creates impact."
- "I am a good steward of what I have and will continue to be for the wealth that is coming."

Remember, there is nothing wrong with you if you want more. You *should* want more!

You can want more and still be deeply generous. You can receive and uplift others. You can be wildly abundant and inherently good. None of those are mutually exclusive. You believe what you choose to believe, so decide wisely. Abundance doesn't change your character—it magnifies it. And you, my friend, were made for this.

Personal Work

Grab your journal and dig into these prompts:

- What did I learn about money growing up? What did I hear (explicitly or implicitly) about rich people?
- Was I ever told it was selfish to want more? By whom?
- What does having money make me afraid of? And why?
- If I had financial freedom, who might disapprove? And why? Do I agree with those old beliefs about money (the responses to the above questions)?
- Are they serving me? If not, am I ready and willing to change them?
- If I had financial freedom, who would benefit?
- How would that make me feel?
- What would I do with more money?
- How would it feel to use it in ways that align with my values?

Then release them: Write down every old belief that no longer serves you, using this format: "I release the belief that...."

Examples: "I release the belief that rich people are bad." "I release the belief that I should only want what I need." "I release the belief that I have to earn money through struggle." "I release the belief that there will never be enough."

Next, read through your list and find the opposite for each statement. Write down those positives on a new sheet of paper in this format: "I believe I will be a good steward of my upcoming wealth." "Having more money will not change me—it will elevate my purpose and be a blessing to myself and others." "I believe that anything I want I can have and deserve." "I believe that money comes to me easily." "I believe that there will always be plenty of money for me and my family."

Once you've written down all your new beliefs, burn the first paper—the one with all the beliefs you are releasing. Read them out loud, then throw the paper into the fire, and watch it burn. You don't need to hold onto those anymore.

Rewrite Your Money Story

Now that you've identified and intentionally released those old beliefs, it's important to write your new money story. This is so important because you are now taking the time to identify what you want *instead.* And like we've always talked about, this step is key to getting new results.

Here are some journal prompts to guide you:

- I believe that abundance is...
- I believe I am...
- The kind of wealth I want to build is...
- How will money change my life for the better?

- Why do I want more money in my life?
- Who will I be with wealth and financial freedom?

Now that you've taken the time to understand what has been blocking your flow of abundance in the past and causing some of your self-sabotaging behaviors, lean into this new story. Read it daily. Remind yourself of how and why you want to manifest abundance and continue working to change those old, limiting beliefs.

Chapter 18

Money Mindset Q&A

How Do I Stop Sabotaging My Money Goals?

Self-sabotaging behaviors are a response to our inherent beliefs about money. So do your personal work—journal to find out what those beliefs are. Why don't you believe that you deserve money? Are you good with money or capable of growing your money? Do you believe you can grow your money into wealth? If not, why not?

What are your behaviors with money? Do you spend it the second you get it? What do you spend it on? Why do you do that? What are you afraid will happen if you don't spend or save it right away? Are you obsessed with saving money? That can also be a form of lack. So, why just save? Why not invest and grow?

If you hold on tight to money, why? Where does that come from?

Asking yourself these questions will help you find your self-sabotaging behaviors and identify why they don't serve you, so that you can change them. Then use Mental Tennis the way you've done above to change those beliefs.

Remember that when you use your offensive tools around money, your thoughts begin to change, which will influence your actions, which will then change your results—which finally will change the belief. So, these mottos and affirmations will do serious work if you remain consistent.

Why Is It So Hard to Receive Money?

Receiving is often the hardest part. Think of all the times you've blocked it in the past, the times when someone offered to pick up the check, but you insisted. Now, I'm not saying never insist on picking up a check, but just ask yourself: Was that your default setting?

Do you refuse help when it's offered? "Oh no, that's okay, I got it. Thanks anyway though." Ever said that? I know I sure used to. Ever declined a compliment when it was given? When someone says something like, "I love that outfit on you!" and you've replied, "Oh this? It was on sale at Target; it was nothing!" Um, yeah.

All of those little ways you deflect are also little ways you deflect abundance. If you are blocking the flow of good in any form, it's jamming up your abundance signal too. So practice receiving all things with grace and gratitude. If a compliment is given, say thank you and give one back. Practice that abundant flow of positive energy—and you'll get better at recognizing and receiving abundance too.

Power Mottos: Here are some examples:

- "I am open and receptive to all the goodness the Universe has to offer!"
- "I am receiving all good things!"
- "I am receiving wealth and abundance and couldn't be happier about it! I am aware of all the good in my life and excited to receive more."

How Do I Stop Thinking There's Never Enough?

This is pretty simple—not easy, but simple. It's just an old belief; one we change using Mental Tennis and Power Mottos. Consistency will reverse that belief over time. I've provided tons of those in this book, so go through and find the ones that speak to you, or better yet, write your own so they will be customized to annihilate your limiting belief.

I will always have everything I need to provide a beautiful life for myself and my family. Abundance is on its way!

How Do I Manifest More Money When I Have a Salary Job?

This is a question I get all the time. And the answer might feel a little frustrating at first: You don't worry about the *how*. I know, that probably sounds crazy. But stay with me. The truth is, I don't know exactly how more money will show up for you right now. And no matter how hard you try to figure it out, you'll likely reach the same conclusion. It's uncomfortable, I get it. But that's how it is—and accepting this is where your biggest mind shift will take place. The more you fight this reality the more you block the flow of abundance.

You could spend weeks overthinking this, trying to "solve" the riddle and still end up nowhere. That's exactly why you need to set that part aside. The *how* is not your job. It is outside your control. Your focus should be on what you *can control*, and that's where your creative energy needs to stay.

Remember when we talked about separating what's in your control from what isn't? This is the moment to lean into that. You don't control how or when more money shows up. Obsessing over it not only drains you, it creates "struggle energy" which is the opposite of what we want. The how isn't your responsibility. That's the Universe's role. It makes up the 25 percent of the manifesting equation that's beyond your reach, beyond logic, and not something you can force. Your job is to stay focused on the part you *can* influence—your thoughts, your energy, and your actions.

Instead of fixating on what we can't control, we shift our focus to what we *can*. Are you actively working to change your limiting beliefs around money? Are you doing the personal work from earlier chapters to clear the blocks that have been holding you back? Are you using your mindset tools daily to call in abundance? Are you being a responsible steward of the money you already have? Are you following through on the practical steps—applying for that new role, positioning yourself for a promotion, getting your resume out there, staying open to inspired ideas and unexpected opportunities? Are you building relationships and leveraging your current resources to move forward? Are you daily focusing on gratitude instead of lack?

If you're doing all of that, then you're doing your part. You're focused on your 75 percent—the part that's within your control. And the return on that effort will come when you least expect it, often from a source you didn't see coming.

It will start to show up in one of three ways. First, as an opportunity—so keep your eyes and mind open to possibilities that may not look exactly how you expected. Second, as an inspired idea—so stay tuned in and pay attention when a thought lights you up or nudges you to take action. And third, as unexpected "money ain't a thing" moments—a concept I first shared in *Hustle Believe Receive*—where abundance shows up as unexpected discounts, gifts, or things being paid for, just like the examples we've already covered.

Let me be clear. Every single client I've worked with who was on a fixed income, meaning a set salary, has manifested more money by using the *Think It* tools. Every single one. And these aren't small wins. I've had clients who never would have applied for a promotion before doing this work, go after it, and land not just one but multiple promotions. Some weren't even looking for a new job, but when the opportunity showed up, they stepped out in faith and negotiated the highest salary package of their life—something they never would have had the confidence to pursue in the past. Others received unexpected bonuses from companies that had never offered them before. Some were granted stock options or profit-sharing that paid out far beyond what they imagined. One client received a sizable and unexpected buyout that allowed him to retire early. Others inherited money they didn't see coming or became the unexpected recipient of surprise income. The list is long. The bottom line is this: The tools work when you stay consistent and focus on what you *can control.*

Power Mottos: Here are a few examples, but don't forget to write your own.

- "I don't know how or when, but abundance is coming!"
- "I am controlling my controllables and happily let the how and when go!"
- "Whenever and however the money comes, I will celebrate it with joy and gratitude!"

Client Example: Susan is a client who had a great corporate job but was still living paycheck to paycheck because of some limiting money beliefs and self-sabotaging behaviors. This is super common and a frustrating place to be, so we used the *Think* It tools to rewire her thinking and beliefs. Within the first year of working together, she was offered a new job with a $24,000 annual pay increase.

Over our next eighteen months of coaching, she was recruited again and offered another job with an annual salary increase of an additional $28,000. Six months after starting that new role, there were some shifts in her department, and she was offered a promotion with a sizable raise, a retroactive bonus, and profit share. To date, she has increased her annual income (since she started working with me and using these tools) by over $80,000 annually! I'd say that's some serious return on investment.

It's not chump change. It's not fluff or BS. If it can work for her, it can work for you. But every single one of those came as an opportunity—not always one she was comfortable with or even eager to receive or accept. We worked on those beliefs each time using these tools so that her confidence and "imposter syndrome" didn't block the opportunities, and she was able to take action to receive the abundance she'd asked the Universe to deliver.

So be open. What you're asking for is going to require you to get uncomfortable. It's going to push you to step into your greatness, so don't let old beliefs prevent you from getting everything you want.

Can I Manifest More Money If I Am in Debt?

Yes. Full stop. Yes. And you can manifest being debt-free. Use Mental Tennis, Power Mottos, and your I AM statements to get your mindset aligned with this goal.

Why Do I Get Money, Then Immediately Lose It?

That tracks back to your beliefs associated with self-sabotaging behaviors. Do the "Personal Work" sections from the past examples in this book to see why you are in this negative cycle. What is the belief at the core of this roller coaster? Are you afraid that you'll lose it every time you get it and are thereby creating a self-fulfilling prophecy? Use Power Mottos and Mental Tennis to change that belief.

Money is here to stay, and it feels so good! Money helps me feel safe and secure, and that feels amazing! I am good with money, so I know I'll always have it.

How Can I Manifest Money When My Partner Doesn't Believe in This Stuff?

Your partner's beliefs don't have to match yours for you to manifest what you want. Their doubt doesn't cancel your power—unless you let it. If they question your mindset work or try to poke holes in what you're doing, that's your cue to protect your energy. Use the Energy Bubble and stop discussing money with them.

Your beliefs are still forming. They're tender, and doubt—especially from someone close to you—can shake them. It's okay to keep this part of your journey sacred. You don't need their agreement to succeed. Make a quiet promise to yourself that you'll show them through results. Let the abundance speak for itself. And if they benefit from it too, great. If not...well, it might raise a different question entirely. Just something to sit with.

Calm Mindset

Reduce Stress, Ease Anxiety, and Protect Your Energy

Chapter 19

How Do I Calm My Mind?

What to Do When You Can't "Turn It Off"

You know that feeling when your mind just won't stop? Your body might be still, but inside, your thoughts are speeding—loud, chaotic, relentless. You're replaying that awkward email, worrying about money, stressing over your kid's behavior, and mentally mapping your next year…all at once. That's real-life stress. And if you don't catch it, it builds fast and turns into full-blown anxiety.

This is where the Power of Pause becomes essential. It's how you interrupt the noise before it becomes a negative manifesting spiral.

Real Life Example: You're lying in bed, almost asleep, when suddenly you remember that work email you forgot to send. Now your mind is racing through your entire to-do list, your finances, and every what-if scenario imaginable. Your chest tightens, your heart rate jumps, and sleep slips away.

What to do: Grab your phone and record a quick voice note, getting out whatever your brain is holding onto. Just the act of dumping those thoughts gives your mind permission to let go. Once the noise is out of your head, you can finally use the Power of Pause to quiet your system and come back to calm.

Power of Pause: Example

Step 1: Recognize the Thought

Okay, that just triggered my feelings of stress and overwhelm. I'm going to do something about it. (The phone brain-dump above.)

Step 2: Pause the Thought

This is not the time, right now I need sleep.

Step 3: Identify What You Want Instead

I release this stress and am choosing to get a good night's rest.

Step 4: Change the Subject

Mentally walk yourself through a moment that makes you feel peaceful, like a beautiful beach vacation. Imagine yourself feeling happy and carefree, watching someone you love laugh and smile while playing in the waves. Who's with you? How do you feel? Why does it feel so good? Just let your mind leisurely drift into this happy fantasy. Remember, it's doing more than just calming you in the moment—it's creating that moment for you to manifest in your future!

Step 5: Agree to Address It

In the morning, keep your promise to yourself. Listen to the voice note and take care of the things you need to deal with. Get them off your to-do list first thing in the morning. This trains your brain to trust you. You're showing it that the thought is not being ignored—it's just being trained not to take over your mental space at a time when you can do nothing to solve it. It's also proving to yourself that you can complete the needed tasks quickly and address things without procrastinating. The more you build this trust, the less all those crazy thoughts will haunt you, because they know that now you have a process for follow-through that works.

Power Motto Examples

"I'm excited for a great night's sleep. I get shit done!"

- "I'll handle it in the morning. I control what is within my power, and I let the rest go."
- "I am proud of myself for following through. I am proud of myself for keeping my word."

Pro Tip

Put on a guided meditation for rest and relaxation on YouTube. There are thousands of amazing sleep meditations or sleep meditation music options that you can run all night to help improve your sleep and train your brain to disconnect and rest. Make sure your settings are adjusted so that another video won't automatically play when yours is finished. Do your happy visualization (the "Change the Subject" step above) with this playing quietly in the background. Meditations like this also help rewire our subconscious, which is most impressionable and active when we are drifting into sleep and while asleep, so use this to your advantage by playing one that will help change some of the beliefs you've worked on in previous chapters.

Chapter 20

How Do I Stop a Negative Spiral?

What to Do When Something Spins You Out

One stressful text and suddenly your whole day is thrown off. Your nervous system kicks into overdrive—you feel shaky, irritable, angry, or completely shut down. You start obsessing over how to respond, replaying the conversation in your head, arguing with them silently. Before you know it, your mind is spinning, and you can't focus on anything else.

This is the moment to use Mental Tennis. It's your tool to interrupt the spiral and take back control of your thoughts.

Real Life Example: You open your email and see a passive aggressive message from your boss. Without even thinking, your mind jumps to panic: *I'm not doing good enough. I'm going to get fired. I'll never find another job.*

Mental Tennis:

See It: Recognize those thoughts (in other words, hear yourself): *Wait a second. What am I saying?*
Stop It: *That's not true!*
Replace It: *I am good at my job. I bring a ton of value to my role. My job is safe.*

You're not avoiding the situation or those feelings. You're not slapping a generic "positive attitude" Band-Aid on it. You're regaining control of your emotions and reactions in a moment that was about to spin you out. And you are reinforcing the outcomes you actually want. It's a huge difference.

Power Mottos: Here are a few examples of effective Power Mottos, but don't forget to write ones the specifically address your situation.

- "I no longer make negative assumptions; I can ask for clarification."
- "I refuse to take this personally and let it ruin my day."
- "No one has the power to affect my energy, unless I let them. I will not let this get to me."
- "I am good at my job."

You can use this same process anytime something or someone triggers you that would normally send you into a spiral. Instead of letting those thoughts take over your headspace, you interrupt them by responding directly. Push back with a firm, *That's not true,* and then replace the thought with what you want instead.

See it. Stop it. Replace it.

Chapter 21

Why Am I So Anxious All the Time?

What to Do When Fear or Anxiety Show Up for "No Reason"

This is incredibly common. Your life might feel stable on the outside, but your body doesn't feel safe. Anxiety doesn't always need a logical reason—it only needs a trigger. Often, it's tied to old wiring or past experiences that haven't been fully cleared, like we discussed in part 1.

Real Life Example: You're driving. Everything seems fine, but suddenly your chest feels tight, and your stomach is in knots. There's no obvious reason. Just that low hum of dread running underneath it all.

Identify the Thought: Even when it feels like the anxiety came out of nowhere, there is always a thought behind it. It might be a nearly subconscious reaction to something that happened earlier, or a thought so quick you didn't fully notice it.

But if you take a moment and look a little deeper, the root is always there. It just takes some self-awareness to uncover it.

Ask Yourself: *What was I thinking about an hour ago while I was doing that task? What has been on my mind today or throughout the week? What am I afraid of right now? Where is this fear coming from? When did I start feeling this way?*

This reflection can be a powerful way to uncover the source of your emotional reaction. Often, what feels like a sudden wave of stress or anxiety is really your body trying to bring something suppressed to the surface, something that is ready to be acknowledged and released. You can't change what you haven't identified, so when these emotions show up, pause and examine them. Try to trace them back to the root thought.

Your mind uses your body to get your attention. That tight chest, that pit in your stomach—it's a signal. Instead of ignoring it, lean in. This is part of your healing. Once you understand the thought behind the feeling, you can remind yourself that you no longer need that protective response. You are no longer in danger. You are growing, healing, and letting go of the beliefs that no longer serve you.

Use Your I AM Statements: Speak directly to your nervous system with clear, grounding words. Try saying:

"I am safe. I am protected."

"I am in control of how I feel."

"I am healing."

"I am releasing what no longer serves me."

"I am ___________." *(Fill in the blank with the opposite of the fear or emotion you just uncovered.)*

Change the Narrative: Once the I AM Statements begin to calm your body and quiet your mind, guide yourself into a more empowered story. Speak it clearly and with intention. You might say something like:

"I know it felt scary to experience that sense of __________ again, but I'm grateful it surfaced. It showed me what I'm ready to release. I no longer need to feel __________, because now I am __________. I am healing. I am growing. I am letting go of this fear, this worry, this anxious thought. It no longer belongs to me. I am safe."

Power Mottos: Here are some examples…

- "I am safe and protected."
- "I have the power to control how I feel, anytime, anywhere."
- "I am letting go of what no longer serves me. I am ready to receive all the joy, calm, and happiness that is coming into my life."
- "I am actively changing old habits and creating a new life."
- "I am transforming every day. I am learning and growing every day."

Chapter 22

How Do I Stop Obsessing Over Things I Don't Control?

How to Shift Your Focus

This is where anxiety lives—in the space between what matters to you and what you can't control. Most of us spend so much mental energy fixating on things we have no power to change while convincing ourselves we can. That, to me, is the very definition of anxiety. If I'm pouring all my focus into a problem that's outside my control, of course I'm going to feel overwhelmed.

The tricky part is, we often don't realize we're doing it. It feels like we're being productive or preparing for the worst, but really, we're just feeding fear.

Real Life Example: You finally land an interview for your dream job, and instead of feeling excited, you're consumed by fear. *What if I mess it up? What if I don't get it?*

Identify the Thought: *I'm afraid I won't get the job I really want.*

What to Use: This is where your Power Mottos come in. They're your go-to tool for shifting that inner dialogue and grounding back into belief.

What Do You Control?

Grab a piece of paper and a pen. Yes, actually do it. You can't sort this out entirely in your head. Writing it down helps your brain recalibrate and see things more clearly.

Draw a line down the middle of the page. At the top of one side, write: *Things I Control.* Then start listing them.

You control whether your resume is strong and current. You control how prepared you are for the interview and whether you've done your research. You control how you dress, how you present yourself, and the energy you bring into the room. You control your follow-up and your professionalism.

You also control the story you tell yourself about how it went. You decide whether you build yourself up or tear yourself down. You control how you feel during and after the interview—whether you stay optimistic or let doubt take over. That part is yours.

What Do You NOT Control?

Now, look at the other side of your paper and label it: *Things I Don't Control.* Start listing everything that's outside your power.

You don't control whether you are the exact fit they are looking for.

You don't control whether they personally clicked with you or liked you.

You don't control if another candidate has more experience or qualifications.

You don't control whether they call you back.

You don't control whether you get the job.

Now that you can clearly see the difference, you can shift your energy. Focus it entirely on what you *do* control. And any time your mind starts drifting back to the things on this list, that's your signal to use your Power Mottos and bring your thoughts back to your lane.

Power Mottos: Here are a few samples of how you'd create effective Power Mottos for this example.

- "I've done everything in my power to get this job. If it's right for me, the offer will come."
- "I trust that I will land the job that aligns with my purpose. If this one is meant for me, it will be mine."

I've helped so many clients manifest their dream jobs. The path isn't always easy or predictable, but it always works out in their favor when they stay aligned and committed to the process. These mottos are here to help you let go of what you can't control and stay grounded in belief. They are your reminder that the right opportunity will find you, even if it's not this one. Keep trusting. Keep going.

Maybe this really was your dream job. Or maybe it was a lesson in disguise. The truth is, only God or the Universe knows which it was. If you get the offer, it's because it was meant for you. And if you don't, trust that something bigger is at play. The Universe was protecting you from something that wasn't aligned and was preparing you for what is. That entire interview process helped sharpened your skills, boosted your confidence, and helped you get ready. And now, when the right opportunity shows up, you'll be more than ready to step into it fully.

Here is where we trust the process. It will not let you down. Keep the faith no matter the outcome, and the perfect opportunity will come.

Stress and anxiety no longer run the show. You now have tools that allow you to interrupt the spiral, calm your nervous system, and redirect your energy to create what you want. Whether it's the Power of Pause to manage everyday stress, Mental Tennis to break out of a thought loop, or Power Mottos to shift how you feel in real time—you're equipped to change your future results.

Keep using these tools until they become second nature. The more you practice, the more peace and clarity you'll feel. And when life throws something hard your way again, because it will, you won't just endure it or wait for it to pass. You'll know how to face it in the moment and respond in a way that moves your life forward.

Chapter 23

How Can I Stop Being So Triggered?

How to Regulate Your Emotional Reactions

Real Life Example: A message from someone instantly triggers you. Maybe it's an email from your boss whose passive aggressive tone always gets under your skin. It could also be a text from a coworker, a family member, or anyone whose name popping up already makes your chest tighten. You dread opening it because you already know how it's going to make you feel.

Here's how to apply your tools:

Energy Bubble: Before you open the message, take a moment to protect your energy. Close your eyes, take a deep breath, and imagine yourself surrounded by a calm, protective bubble. Then say your Power Motto out loud:

"No one has the power to affect my energy or ruin my day unless I let them. And I'm not about to let them."

Say it a few times, taking slow deep breaths in between. This gives your nervous system a moment to reset so you can stay in control before you even read a single word.

Use Your I AM Statements: Mentally repeat a few of your grounding I AM Statements to center yourself and reinforce how you want to feel in this moment. Remind yourself of who you are and what you know to be true.

Say to yourself:

"I am in control of my emotions."

"I know I'm great at my job."

"I don't need to take this personally."

"I am steady and confident, no matter what someone else says or does."

Now, do your best to read the message with neutrality. Avoid adding tone, meaning, or assumptions. Read it as if it came from a stranger—without emotional weight or attachment. Pause. Breathe.

Talk Yourself Through It: If something in the message still stirs you, acknowledge it without letting it take over. Remind yourself that your reaction might be tied to old patterns or past experiences. Maybe you braced for criticism before even opening the message. If that's true, give yourself a moment to check in.

Ask Yourself:

Is this a reaction or a response?

Could I be assuming negative intent that may not even be there?

Can I read this with a neutral lens?

Is there a question I could ask instead of making an assumption?

You're not just reacting anymore—you're actively choosing how to respond. And that is real emotional regulation in action.

Keep guiding your internal dialogue instead of letting it run on autopilot. Talk to yourself the way you'd talk to your child or someone you love. Say: *I don't need to take this personally.*

I am not letting this affect my energy. Everyone loves me, including my boss. I'm great at what I do, and I love my job. I choose to respond with calm and clarity, then move on with my day.

This does not deserve more energy than I'm willing to give it.

Get in the habit of assuming nothing.

This applies to all human interaction. It's often our assumptions that cause the most damage. When in doubt, ask questions. And if you do find yourself assuming, choose to assume positive intent. I learned this from my partner early in our relationship, and I love it. We made it a commitment in our communication—to always assume the best in each other—and I can honestly say it has been a game-changer. It keeps our connection honest, open, and safe. And it works just as well in work and everyday life too.

However, if something in the message crossed a boundary or felt inappropriate, it's important to address it. That doesn't mean reacting impulsively or brushing it off. It means responding with calm and clarity. This is where the Energy Bubble technique becomes especially helpful. It allows you to regulate your emotional response so you can speak up without escalating the situation.

Instead of assuming negative intent, just ask. You might say something like, "I understand what you're saying in the first part, but could you clarify what you meant by the second part?"

Approaching a difficult person in this way is incredibly disarming. It shifts the energy, especially if there has been tension or conflict in the past. It dissolves that underlying pressure and creates space for more honest, respectful communication.

Chapter 24

How Do I Keep Other People's Energy from Ruining My Day?

How to Protect Your Mental Space

Real Life Example: You're having a decent day, and then your partner walks in the door with a short tone and irritated energy. Without thinking, you start bracing for conflict. Maybe you get defensive, snap back, or begin shutting down and internalizing their mood.

Here's how to apply your tools:

Energy Bubble: Step into another room, even if just for a moment, and bring your attention inward. Take a few slow, deep breaths. Visualize your protective energy bubble surrounding you—calm, strong, and grounded. Let yourself feel it. This will help you pause before reacting. That quick comeback you were about to make? That's the *old* you. That instinct to armor up or emotionally check out? That's the old version of you too. You're not doing that anymore. You're learning a new response. So breathe, center yourself, and choose how you want to show up next.

We are learning how to have healthy communication, we're becoming self-aware and growing, and we're showing up differently, making new choices.

This all happens in a matter of seconds, so you can definitely do this—I don't wanna hear those objections! You can even do it if you're sitting in the car with your partner. Just close your eyes, talk to yourself, and get in your bubble.

Power Motto: Say it…"No one has the power to affect my energy unless I let them."

Assume Positive Intent: Instead of reacting to the voice in your head that might be blasting a few of these thoughts—*Oh, here they go again, being a dick!* or *I'm done with their attitude!*—which are assuming the worst and would escalate the situation, can you ask a question instead?

Say to yourself, *I know they are not a jerk. They probably didn't even realize they snapped at me. They care about me. Let me see what's wrong.* And then ask them: "Are you okay? Can you tell me what happened today?"

Note: All of this applies under the assumption that you're in a relationship you want to be in, and that for the most part, it's a healthy one. If it's not—if you're experiencing verbal or physical abuse—that is a completely different situation. That is *not* where we assume positive intent. In that case, I want you to use your Power Mottos and I AM Statements to give yourself the strength and clarity to walk away. Please hear me when I say this: I love you. I may never know you personally, but the fact that you are reading this book means something. It means you matter. It means your life, your well-being, your voice—all of it—is important.

You deserve to be respected. You deserve to be loved and cherished for exactly who you are.

If that is not your reality, please seek help. Reach out to someone you trust. You are not alone. We get one life, and it is too short to spend it with someone who disrespects you, diminishes you, or causes you harm. You are worthy of so much more. Never settle for less than love that feels safe.

People always ask me, "How could you just kick your husband out when you found out he was having an affair? Didn't you fight for your marriage?" They look at me like I'm a monster with nine heads. No, I did not fight for that man. And no, I have never regretted that decision for one second. I know my worth, and I know that I could never love someone who was capable of that kind of betrayal and who was living a double life.

To be clear, I am well aware that this is not a decision most people in my shoes would make, and that's okay—I get it. I respect the decisions of those who choose to stay in situations like mine, but I also support anyone who wants out, who knows they deserve better, and who makes that choice.

Chapter 25

How Do I Get Out of a Funk?

How to "Shake It Off" and Get Positive Momentum Going

We've all been there—that space where forward momentum disappears, life starts to feel heavy and repetitive, and motivation is nowhere to be found. It's not that anything is terribly wrong, but nothing feels exciting or inspiring either. It's that low, *mehhh* energy that slowly pulls your vibe down.

Most people try to ride it out. They wait, hoping that tomorrow will feel different or that something good will happen to lift their spirits. But with each day that passes, they feel more disconnected from their energy, more stuck in their mindset, and more powerless to shift their circumstances. That wait-and-see cycle is draining. I've been there more times than I can count, and I know how frustrating it is when you want change but feel like you can't access the energy to make it happen.

Because I've never been one to sit around waiting for things to change—especially when they're outside my control—I made a decision years ago to create a simple action plan I could use to pull myself out of those low-energy lulls. It's helped me stay in motion, even when things feel stagnant, and avoid getting stuck in that space for too long. I've shared these exact steps with clients for more than a decade, and they work every time.

Step 1: Guided Meditation

Start with a guided meditation focused on energy clearing or cleansing. I personally love Reiki Rachel's sessions on YouTube, especially her energy cleanse and chakra balancing meditations. There are plenty of great options available, so find one that resonates with you.

These meditations are powerful for releasing heavy, stuck, or low energy. Clearing that emotional clutter makes the next steps more effective and easier to apply. I try to do this as soon as I notice something feels off, even if it's in the middle of the day. I'll pause, take a thirty-minute break, and find a quiet space to reset.

This one step alone helps prevent low energy from building momentum and unraveling the mindset work I've already done.

Step 2: Get Grateful

When you're in a mental funk, it's usually because your focus has drifted toward everything that feels wrong or out of sync. And when that becomes your focus, it's no surprise that your energy drops. What we focus on grows. So if your thoughts are centered on lack, doubt, fear, or frustration, those feelings expand and the path forward feels harder to see. That cycle creates even more resistance and keeps you feeling stuck.

The most effective way to shift this energy is through gratitude. I stop what I'm doing and start listing everything I'm thankful for. As you make your list, take a moment to really feel the presence of each thing in your life. Let yourself sit in the feeling of appreciation—for the people, experiences, resources, and even small moments that bring joy or stability.

This practice will stop the downward spiral and help replace it with hope, possibility, and a more balanced perspective. It reminds you of what is already working and begins to change your momentum in a powerful way.

Make this gratitude practice a daily habit for at least seven days. You'll likely notice a shift within the first twenty-four hours, and the momentum will continue to build each day as you keep your focus on what's already good in your life. The more you lean into thankfulness, the better you'll feel.

Step 3: Use Mental Tennis

When a negative thought shows up, respond to them immediately. Use Mental Tennis to challenge and replace them with the outcome you want. See it. Stop it. Replace it.

Step 4: Use Power Mottos

Start shifting the narrative around whatever pulled you into the funk. Focus your thoughts on what you *do* want, rather than what you don't. Each morning, before your feet hit the floor, take a moment to decide how you want to feel. Tell yourself, "I love my life!" Think about what you're grateful for and what you're excited to welcome into your life. Say your mottos out loud. Say them often. This sets the tone for your day and helps rewrite the story you've been telling yourself.

Success Mindset

Level Up Your Career and Achieve Your Goals

Chapter 26

How Do I Advance My Career or Change Paths When I Feel Stuck?

How to Create the Career (and Life) You Really Want

IRL Example: You're feeling stuck in a job you've outgrown, and every time you think of change, you panic. You've been in the same role for a while. You're good at it. You've even built some success. But lately…you're burned out. You dread Mondays, and no matter how much you earn or achieve, you still feel unfulfilled.

You catch yourself daydreaming about doing something completely different—maybe starting your own thing, pivoting into a creative role, or finally applying to work in a field that lights you up. But then the fear floods in: *What if I fail? What if I can't replace my income? What will people think if I walk away from a "good" job?*

Ask yourself, *What do I want instead?*

Daydreaming: To help identify the desire of your heart, ask yourself what do you want? Close your eyes and see yourself loving a job—it doesn't need to be your current job or any specific job, just imagine a world where you love a job. What about it do you love? What's different from your current job and work life? What makes it so great? What does your day look like? How do you feel when you log in or show up? What kind of impact are you having? Why do you want something different? Grab your journal and write down those answers. What is making you feel stuck right now? How long have you felt this way? What are your regular thoughts regarding your job or career?

See how you dress, how you speak, how you lead. See your name on that door, on that book, on that team roster. What about this visual is exciting for you? What is scary? Why? If you could get paid amazingly for doing anything you love, what are some things you love?

This journaling process is designed to get you unlocked so that your creative juices flow—it's not intended to magically lead you to your next perfect job. That will come as an opportunity after you've taken the time to identify what matters to you, how you want to live, what you want, and why it's important. Those ideas and opportunities will come when your energy, mind, and heart are open to receiving them. That's what this intentional journaling helps reveal. So try not to judge it or force it—just let whatever answers pop up land on the page.

More Journal Prompts: What's next? What is no longer working in your current career or life chapter? What do you secretly wish you were doing instead? What story are you telling yourself about why you can't have it? Whose voice is that—yours or someone else's? What does "success on my terms" look like? What's one thing you could do this week that the confident version of you would do?

Here's how to use these tools to get unstuck:

Mental Tennis: Example

See It: *I'm thinking that I can't have a rewarding career because it would be irresponsible, and because I would probably fail.*
Stop It: *Stop! That's an old belief. I'm working hard to be open and receptive to creating a life I love. I deserve to have a job I love too!*
Replace It: *What if I succeed? What if I'm more successful than I ever imagined possible? What if I make way more money and this move was totally worth the risk? I don't care what other people think; I have confidence in my decisions.*

Power Mottos: Repeat these when you feel stuck, unsure, or like playing small:

- "I'm ready for my next chapter."
- "I believe I can have a career I love and make great money doing it."
- "Opportunities come to me, and I trust myself and take aligned action."
- "I trust myself to grow, pivot, and thrive when the opportunity comes."
- "I trust my gut and make good decisions."
- "I am allowed to want more—and go after it."
- "I build success on my terms."
- "What I want wants me back."

- "I am becoming the version of me who has already done this."

Action Step: Write down one tiny step you can take this week to explore your next chapter. Not a full pivot—just a simple starting point. Nothing happens without action, so it's important for us to put some muscle behind our desires and start flushing out some of our new ideas. Think about all the things you can control and write them down—see on paper just how many options you have. There is more than you think; I can promise you that.

Here are some examples of simple things you can do to continue getting unstuck: Message someone in a role you admire and ask for a fifteen-minute convo. Write down the story of your future life and why you want it. Update your LinkedIn or resume with language that reflects where you want to go—not just where you've been. Join a class, group, or mastermind session aligned with the life/career you want to create. Do a little research, but not too much; it will kill your dreams! Fill a Pinterest board with what that new life and career looks like visually.

Taking one step unlocks the next.

Don't underestimate the power of creating momentum.

Chapter 27

How Do I Manage a Toxic Workplace?

How to Transform Your Work Experience

If what we focus on expands, then every time you say you hate your job, your boss, or a coworker, you're feeding that energy. You're reinforcing the negativity and making it harder to shift the situation. That mindset adds fuel to the fire and helps the toxicity grow.

Now here's the hard truth: If you've been in more than one toxic work environment, you are likely participating in the dynamic in some way.

Ouch. I know that's not easy to hear. You probably hate reading this. You might even want to throw this book across the room or leave a nasty comment online. But I'm not here to sugarcoat it. I've coached far too many people through these exact patterns to avoid saying what needs to be said.

If you've had serious clashes with bosses or coworkers at more than one job, it's time to take an honest look at the pattern. Because it wasn't *all* them. Some of that energy was coming from you too. People respond to energy—especially the kind we're not even aware we're giving off. You might think the message you sent was polite or simply direct, but what they received may have felt sharp, passive, or dismissive. And sometimes, it's the other way around.

I've coached so many professionals, from corporate executives to mid-level employees, who were convinced that the chaos in their work environments was entirely someone else's fault. But when we did the work to shift their energy, the change around them was almost immediate. Energy is contagious. And when yours shifts, so does the response you get.

Client Example: I was brought in to work with a corporate team that was deep in dysfunction. The environment was toxic, and everyone had issues with everyone else. Naturally, each person thought *they* were not the problem—they just wanted me to "fix" someone else on the team.

Yeah, it was quite the assignment. Imagine walking into a room full of type-A leaders, egos running high, and trying to tell them they might be contributing to the issue. Cue a little Taylor Swift, and ask yourself, *am I the problem here?* I'll be honest, it was a challenge. I had to strike a balance between keeping the atmosphere open and bringing the truth to the table, because without that, there's no path forward.

What I told them was simple: You only control you. You control the energy you bring into every meeting, every email, every conversation. And that energy is either clashing with others—creating resistance, triggering defensiveness, frustration, or anger—or it's creating a space for open dialogue, creativity, fresh ideas, and a cohesive team dynamic.

Defensiveness arises when we bring an energy or communication style that triggers the other person's need to defend, recede, or protest. If that is *not* the energy we bring, then we typically won't get that response from people. If you're bringing a collaborative spirit, open mind, safe communication style, and a willingness to learn—and have checked your ego at the door—you will stop getting met with toxic behaviors. Maybe not immediately, but they will recede because that fire will no longer have the oxygen it needs to survive.

By choosing to change the energy *you bring*, you can impact the energy of others in a positive way, thereby creating the type of environment that is healthier for everyone.

By focusing on solutions, listening, openness, safe communication, and being willing to learn and adapt, you can create a mentally healthy workplace for yourself—regardless of what other people do.

You can choose to not stoke the flames of negativity and toxicity by disengaging from those conversations and not perpetuating those narratives. Over time, people will interact with you differently and respond to you in new, more positive ways. You are more likely to get your desired outcomes by using this approach than you ever would by forcing your way, being defensive, negative, or leading with ego.

Honestly ask yourself these questions: *In the past six months at my job, can I truly say that I've brought positive, open, productive energy each day? Have I encouraged others, spoken highly of them, or given positive reinforcement when it was warranted? Have I focused on finding solutions that work for everyone—or just pushed my own agenda? Have I been open to feedback, suggestions, and criticism—or have I been defensive and accusatory? Have I been self-aware, or have I been focused on everyone else being the problem? Honestly, what kind of energy do I bring to my job, my coworkers, and my boss? Has this served me? What are some things I can work on to improve this and feel more positive about work? How can I focus on me instead of everyone else and everything going on around me? I control me—so let's start controlling me and see what happens!*

This is what I mean by being self-aware and doing personal growth work. It's not an Instagram quote or a trending TikTok. It's real work. It's genuinely being receptive to seeing your behavior, actions, reactions, and current reality in a new light and from a new angle—and that is not easy to do. In fact, most people are incapable of this. I applaud you for reading this and thinking about it, if you've found yourself in a relatable situation. Because it's not easy to take this coaching note, but if you're open to it and willing to make changes, it will dramatically improve your work experience and your working relationships.

This is a *big* deal. Making some simple tweaks to the energy you bring will change everything in your life, not just work, but all your relationships. Instead of sending a subliminal signal that repels people or causes them to negatively interact with you, you'll now be sending a softer one that attracts amazing people, experiences, opportunities, loyalty, and money into your orbit. And those are things we all want, am I right? But sometimes we need a mirror and a willingness to take a thoughtful look at ourselves first, before focusing on everyone else.

The Energy Bubble is how you protect yourself from the negativity and toxicity of others. Use it daily to keep your own vibe positive, open, and unaffected. This deactivates the signals you were sending that caused others to bring that negativity to you or react in unhealthy and triggering ways. Once your side of that equation is deactivated, it's only a matter of time before the overall energy of others slowly begins to soften and shift.

Be responsible for the energy you bring.

How to Deal with Negative or Stressful Thoughts About Work

If this applies to you, shifting your perspective and thoughts around your job is crucial—not only for your mental health but also for your job performance, job security, and future career opportunities. Focusing on the problem will only bring more of that problem, so it's essential to find a new solution and direct your attention toward it moving forward.

Ask Yourself: What stresses you out about work? What's at the root of what you don't like? Is it something you can change? What would be the best-case scenario if it did change? How would you like to feel at work? How would you like to be treated?

Let's say you can't stand someone at work. You probably can't change the fact that you must work together, but what's the best-case scenario? What if you got along with that person? I know—you probably don't *want* to get along with them. You probably just want them gone! But that's not what we're doing here. We're not putting that energy into the Universe.

So, what if there was no tension? What if they didn't annoy you? What if they didn't do *XYZ*? Would that improve your daily work life? What are you grateful for right now as it relates to your job? What is the statement that helps you feel empowered and in control of how you feel as it relates to work?

Here's a sample **Power Motto**:

- "I am grateful for my job and love my team! People are drawn to me at work, and I feel valued, respected, and get along with everyone."

Say your new motto every morning—ten times—before you start work, open your computer, or check your email. Say it between meetings. Say it before you interact with the person or situation that used to bother you. Keep repeating it until whatever frustrated you about your job no longer affects you. This is how you take control of your emotions, reactions, and feelings, preventing yourself from internalizing the challenges of the day. It's a powerful way to protect your mental health.

The most important thing about these mottos is that they are customized to directly address *your* specific fear, worry, or stressor. Your new statement should completely replace the old feeling or belief. By claiming the outcome you want, you begin creating a new mental GPS route—one that gets you off the endless negative roundabout and going in a positive direction full of new outcomes.

Note: I highly recommend the book *How to Win Friends and Influence People* by Dale Carnegie; it gives great insight into these types of work relationships and how to defuse tension.

Chapter 28

Why Do I Procrastinate?

How to Stop Self-Sabotaging and Start Consistently Winning!

IRL Example: You've had the same goal for months…and still haven't started. You've been saying for weeks—maybe months—that you want to start your side hustle. Or begin working out again. Or just clean out your damn closet. This is something you really do want, you know it'll give you energy, confidence, and forward motion. And yet…you keep pushing it off. It's always, "I'll start Monday." But Monday becomes next Monday. Then the first of the month. Then after your birthday. And in the meantime, the guilt and shame build. The negative self-talk gets ruder and louder with each passing day. "What is wrong with you? Why haven't you done it yet?" Know what I mean?

What is procrastination costing you?

For me, this wasn't a new problem, I've always known procrastination was something I needed to work on. But I'd convinced myself it was "a good motivator" because "I'm good under pressure," and "I always get it done in the end." I spent most of my life selling this story to myself and others, believing it was a *strength* in disguise—instead of seeing it for what it really was: intentional self-sabotage.

But something clicked when I read the book *Think and Grow Rich* by Napoleon Hill and saw "procrastination" listed as one of the top reasons why most people fail. That hit different. I suddenly saw all the ways I'd been unintentionally blocking the success I was working so hard to create. *Well shit,* I remember thinking, *if procrastinating is preventing me from getting the rewards of all this work, that's messed up! I don't want that.* So, I set about changing that part of my personality, character, and habits—so I could stop getting in my own way.

Start adding up what procrastination is costing you. Have you been *negatively* manifesting by intentionally putting things off?

What happens when you keep postponing an oil change for your car? You risk incurring possible engine damage and expensive car issues. That thirty-minute, eighty-dollar task could end up costing you thousands. You know this—and yet you still procrastinate. And then you wonder why, when you ask for abundance, you seem to manifest more bills than money…see what I'm sayin'?

Or here's one of mine: I got a parking ticket last summer and stashed it in a drawer intending to pay it later. I meant to—but I forgot. Months passed, and suddenly that sixty-dollar ticket turned into a $240 court notice. Procrastination was literally stealing my abundance!

This same pattern shows up in every area of life—your career, your finances, your health, and your relationships. And the most exhausting part? It's the stress of knowing you haven't done the thing yet. That unfinished task lingers in the back of your mind all day. It doesn't disappear just because you're putting it off. In fact, it does the opposite. Each time it surfaces in your thoughts, it drains more of your mental energy. You start beating yourself up for not taking action. And over time, that builds into chronic, low-grade stress and anxiety that you may not even realize you're carrying. And for what? What are you gaining by avoiding it? Why are you letting it take up so much space?

That doctor's visit you've been meaning to schedule? Those tests you've been avoiding? It's time to make the call. Ask yourself honestly, what's the potential cost of putting it off? Are you asking for health while quietly sabotaging it at the same time? That friend or family member you keep saying you'll "reach out to today"? Do it now. Stop waiting for the right moment and send the text, make the call, write the message. If something were to happen and you never got the chance again, would you be at peace with that? Stop delaying the things you can take care of today. Small actions now can prevent deep regret later.

Separate yourself from the label of procrastination.

Start by separating yourself from the label of procrastination. Stop making it part of your identity. This is a great example of how you might be using I AM Statements in reverse, reinforcing a negative belief you want to change. Every time I caught myself saying, "I'm a procrastinator," I realized I was using it as an excuse to validate the behavior. So, I began shifting it into the past tense. I'd say, "I used to procrastinate, but now I'm learning how to get things off my plate quickly and use my time more efficiently." I started using new I AM Statements like, "I get shit done!" and "I am organized."

Next, focus on building trust with yourself. This takes time, but it's foundational. Every time you follow through and keep a commitment, you're laying down the structure for self-trust. When you can rely on yourself to act without delay, you begin to understand your capacity and what you're capable of completing within a given time frame and what you're not. This will help you to stop overcommitting or saying yes to things that you should not commit to.

Making these small changes relieves so much mental stress. No more constant mental reminders to do the thing. No more running to-do lists repeating in your head. Instead, you're creating a new system—one that supports better habits, stronger follow-through, and more clarity in how you manage your time.

Here are some strategies I've personally implemented and ones I give to my coaching clients to change procrastination habits:

1. Respond in the moment.

   If you open a message—text, email, whatever—*handle it.* If you can't respond right away, don't open it. That unread notification dot will remind you to deal with it later. By creating this new process and sticking to it, you'll begin to trust that you have replied, responded, or dealt with messages that need your attention.
2. Schedule the task.

   If you tell yourself you'll work out, drink water, send the proposal—whatever it is—put it in your calendar or task reminder tool. Then treat it like something you'd show up for. You wouldn't skip a meeting with your boss, so don't skip one with yourself. If my workouts weren't set as recurring meetings in my calendar, I'd never work out. But because they are, that time is always blocked off, and I've trained myself to just get out the door in time for my hot-sculpt yoga class the same way I would if I was meeting a client. By intentionally creating this new scheduled habit, I can now trust myself to know that I will get my workout in four days a week.

3. Do one small thing.

   Procrastination has a bestie named "overwhelm." These are not the types of friends you need in your life. When you learn to take things off your plate that can be done now—rather than putting them on your endless to-do list—you ease the impending sense of overwhelm and feel more productive and in control.

Is there something you've been reminding yourself lately that needs to be done? A dentist appointment to set? A phone call to return? An email waiting for a response? Stop reading and do it right now! Get it off your list—and be proud of yourself for doing it.

Mental Tennis: Use Mental Tennis to reverse the inner dialogue leading to procrastination.

See It: *I'm telling myself to put this task off again.*
Stop It: *I promised I'd stop doing that.*
Replace It: *I can get this done now. I get shit done! I am efficient with my time. I do not put off things I can do right now.*

Do the same for thoughts of guilt and shame associated with not having done it yet. It's important to play Mental Tennis on these thoughts because, left unchecked, they continue to create the identity of a procrastinator and decrease your desire, motivation, or will to change that behavior.

See It: *I'm shaming myself for not getting this done, saying things like, "You're the worst. Why can't you ever just handle shit when you know you need to? You always put things off, and they get worse—what is wrong with you?"*

Stop It: *That is not helpful, and I no longer shame myself because I am learning how to change my behaviors.*

Replace It: *I get shit done! I'm going to take care of this right away. I'm proud of myself for changing and being more organized. I am following through. I complete what I start. I keep my promises to myself.*

Personal Work

Grab your journal and answer these journal prompts to help you uncover how procrastination has been blocking you.

- What are five things I've been procrastinating on recently?
- What has procrastination cost me—financially, emotionally, or in missed opportunities? Write specific examples.
- What do I gain from delaying? What's the payoff?
- What belief is behind this habit? (Examples are "I work better under pressure," "I'm not ready yet," or "I'll fail if I try.")
- What are some new, positive beliefs that would serve me better?

Chapter 29

How Do I Stop Obsessing Over My Weight or Appearance?

How to Improve Your Body Image and Feel Great Starting Now

The #SelfPrideChallenge

I have struggled with my weight and body image since I was twelve years old. I remember being at a friend's house, standing on the digital scale in her bathroom, and seeing "145 lbs." in red on the little backlit reader screen. It's doubtful I had any concept of what those numbers meant, but instinctively I knew they represented something shameful. I didn't dare tell my friend what the scale said, because I knew her number was much lower than mine. She was "good," and I was "bad."

Was it social conditioning? Societal pressure? Nope. It was something instinctive in me. That's what was so grotesquely sick about my young obsession with my body and weight: It wasn't influenced by society or the media. I grew up off the grid, one of six children, with parents who believed the end of the world was imminent and that exposure to anything mainstream would send us directly to hell.

At twelve, I had never seen a magazine, watched TV, listened to secular music, or seen photos of anorexic models (read my childhood memoir *Anomaly* on my Substack called *The Coaching Corner* [@SarahCentrella], and you'll get why). Not only that, but I was raised an organic vegan; we ate only unprocessed food and grew most of what we consumed—so it was healthy eating before there was such a thing. Yet still, I knew I was considered "big-boned" and that being "big" anything made me less than my friends who were naturally small and thin.

Isn't it ridiculous how we come up with these ugly internal stories? I share this because I bet I'm not the only one who carried insanely unhealthy thoughts about body image into adulthood. Maybe you can relate?

Because of all those negative self-thoughts, I found as an adult that no matter what diet or exercise program I tried, nothing ever worked. I could obsessively work out, starve myself, only eat protein, or not touch a carb—but it didn't matter. Nothing ever worked. I baffled trainers. I shocked keto coaches. What could work for "everyone else" never worked for *me.* I finally concluded that no matter what I did, I would never lose weight. After all, I had the proof! A lifetime of it.

So, I gave up entirely for a few years. Just said, *Fuck it. Why bother?* If I could eat a pint of ice cream while binging *Real Housewives* and remain the exact same weight as when I'm psychotically working out and obsessing over what I eat, then why the fuck wouldn't I just eat ice cream?

Three years passed like this, and as I'm sure you've guessed, I felt exponentially worse each year. The number on the scale had barely increased (yes, it's shocking) in all that time, but my body stopped functioning like the body I recognized. I was tired all the time, couldn't think straight to save my life, felt squishy all over, started hiding in the back of photos, stopped showing up for my business, stopped doing fun things with my kids, and couldn't walk up three stairs while holding a conversation. I was a mess.

One day in July 2019, I was relaxing in the sun on my back patio and caught a glimpse of myself in the sliding glass door. I was shocked. It was the first time I saw what I was doing to myself, and it was not cool. *Where is your self-pride, girl?* I thought. I snapped a picture of myself in that reflection, and it's still in my camera roll (under favorites) to this day, because I never want to forget what I looked like—and how I felt—when I let the pride in myself go.

That's when it dawned on me—maybe the reason I could never lose weight was because I truly believed, *No matter what I do, I will never lose weight.* Could it really be that simple? I figured I had nothing to lose. Maybe it was time to change that belief and see what happened.

My transformation began when I realized it wasn't my body holding me back—it was my thoughts and beliefs.

My problem was that my belief and effort were headed in opposing directions. The two were in conflict—which made it impossible to get the results I wanted—until I got them aligned and headed in the same direction. I fixed it by telling myself the outcomes I wanted on repeat, every single day, until I believed them. I changed my thoughts from *I can't lose weight* to *I can lose weight easily* and repeated it so often that eventually my mind replaced the old belief with the new one. Once that new one took root, my results started to match.

I created the #SelfPrideChallenge (www.selfpridechallenge.com), a free mental-and-physical reboot, so my subscribers could join me in getting their mind and body in sync. I wanted to see if changing my internal dialogue around my weight and my body's ability to lose it would change my physical results. In other words, I wanted to see if I could use *Think It* to lose weight and get healthier.

This is all I did; you can do it too:

1. I committed to moving my body for twenty minutes a day. That's it. Not a workout class, not a run, not two hours of cardio—just stand up and move. Most days I did this via walking the dog, but on rainy days I walked intentionally inside my house for twenty minutes or would walk around the grocery store. My only goal was to walk for twenty minutes.
2. I committed to using daily Power Mottos that spoke into existence the outcomes I wanted, built me up, and ultimately would change the belief that I could not lose weight.
3. I committed to drinking eight glasses of water a day.

That's it. It was so much easier than any diet or exercise plan I'd ever tried, and because of that, I was finally able to fully commit. My expectations were not that I'd lose a ton of weight and solve how I felt about my body overnight but that I'd begin to feel physically and mentally *better*.

I knew I could do twenty minutes a day for thirty days—it was manageable. And each day I kept my promise to myself, rising to the challenge and loving the positive feeling of daily accomplishment. My confidence slowly began to build, my energy rejuvenated, my mind cleared up, and the mottos gave me hope, strength, and power. At the end of thirty days, I had shockingly lost nine pounds—the first weight I had lost in nearly a decade.

I've kept those promises to myself ever since. In fact, as I write this and prepare for my fiftieth birthday, I am doing the challenge again, start to finish, but this time adding in a daily workout class so that I can enter my fifties in the best shape of my life! Today I can honestly say that I love my body. I love its flaws. I love that it responds when I consistently take care of it. I love that it is healthy. I love that it looks good and that I feel good in it. I wish I had learned this lesson when I was younger. It would have saved me so much pointless self-hatred.

The good news is that my teenage daughters are growing up in a much different environment. I've taught them from birth to only talk nice to themselves, so they've grown up with the three of us saying things like, "I feel beautiful today!" We give each other compliments constantly, and if one of us slips up and says something negative about how we look, the other will call you out instinctively.

"Hey! We don't say that in this house!" they'll hear me yell down the hall, followed by the universal reminder of "We only say kind and loving things, thank you!"

I'm not going to pretend they'll grow up without body image issues—or even that they don't feel some of that now—but I am proud that we have changed the conversation and shifted the value in our home to who they are, not their weight.

I AM Statements: "I am strong, I am powerful, I am fit." "I am beautiful. I am sexy. I am free!" "I am healthy. I am consistent. I am determined. I am committed. I am amazing!" "I am energetic!"

Power Mottos: Use your mottos to create a new desired outcome for how you want to feel in your body and how you want it to respond; say them every single day. Here are a few examples:

- "I am getting stronger every day!"
- "My body is responding quickly to the work I'm putting in; the weight is falling off!"
- "I love my body! I love myself for consistently showing up!"
- "I am so proud of the work I am putting in; it will pay off!"
- "I am feeling better every day!"
- "I am healthy and full of energy!"
- "I am sexy and confident in my own skin!"

Pro Tip #1

Find an exercise that you enjoy and do it consistently. But set realistic goals you know are achievable. Your body needs to be taken care of—it will work so much better if you give it this respect. Moving your body consistently will clear your mind, help new ideas form, give you inspiration, and make you feel like a sexy bitch—so make it a priority! And vow to never let it be an option again. It's not something you gotta talk yourself in and out of—it's just something you do for you.

Pro Tip #2

Put it in your schedule. Nothing happens these days if it's not in my calendar. That's why I sign up for my barre classes two weeks in advance—that way nothing gets booked over them. I also make sure the class is at the same time every morning, so it becomes a no-brainer habit—just something I do almost on autopilot. Schedule it.

Go sign up for my free #SelfPrideChallenge, and you'll get the motto each morning in your email—created to help you build confidence, encourage you to move your body, and help change the negative beliefs about what you're capable of. It is truly an empowerment challenge, and women from around the world have done it with amazing results—many achieving them multiple times.

It's incredible the connection our thoughts and beliefs have with our physical body. They drive our outcomes, and getting them in sync will help us achieve the results we want.

Chapter 30

Health and Fitness Q&A

Here are some common questions I get from clients when it comes to achieving their health and fitness goals using the *Think It* tools.

How Can Mindset Help Me Stay Consistent with Working Out?

As with everything else we've learned in this book, mindset is the root of our actions. So if our mind is programmed to tell us to skip working out, then gaining consistency is nearly impossible. Consistency comes through showing up and doing the thing you promised to do, one day at a time, and we need our thoughts to prompt and support that action.

It is *not* built by setting an arbitrary goal like, "I'm going to work out for an hour five days a week," if you haven't worked out for an hour in years or done five days a week since your twenties. Instead of making the mistake most people make—overcommitting and under-delivering—do the opposite.

Set a realistic goal—like the one I set to intentionally move my body for twenty minutes a day, knowing that regardless of the day or what it presented, I could always get up and walk around my couch while watching my shows if it came to that. When you set a goal that you know can be accomplished with desire and commitment, you are much more likely to achieve it.

Then focus on one day at a time. Before you go to bed, pull up your schedule for tomorrow and block out time for a thirty-minute walk or your desired workout by putting it on your calendar. That way, you know you can make it happen. When you wake up and go through your schedule for the day, say, "I'm excited to get my workout in today. I've been feeling so good—it'll feel great to keep that momentum going!" Make it something you look forward to throughout the day as your "me time," instead of mentally dreading it.

Power Mottos: Use your mottos to program your mind to *want* to show up. They will start auto-powering you to get your workout done and fuel the belief that you can follow through and achieve anything you set your mind to. When you wake up in the morning, say:

- "I am excited for my workout today—it always feels so great afterward!"
- "I love how I'm showing up for myself! I am feeling fitter, stronger, and more energetic every day."
- "I am consistently proving to myself that I can look and feel my best right now! My body is responding quickly to the work I'm putting in."

I AM Statements: Before your workout, fill your physique with all your positive I AM Statements that will give you power and energy to get the most from your workout. Say things like:

"I am strong. I am powerful!" "I am fit. I am energetic!" "I am sexy!" "I am achieving!" "I am consistent. I am dedicated. I am determined!" "I am healthy. I am motivated!"

How Do I Stay Motivated When I Don't See Results?

Motivation comes from what you tell yourself and your *desire* for a new result—that's it. It's pretty simple. If you've decided that you want a certain outcome, you're more motivated to get it, right? If you don't know what that outcome is, or you're not sure why you want it, then you're "unmotivated" to go after it. If you're feeling unmotivated about your fitness or health goals, it's because you don't know what the real goal is. It's not pounds on a scale, I can pretty much promise you that. It's not a body fat percentage goal, and it's not finishing a marathon. It's something more intangible. And if you don't know what that *is*, you'll procrastinate and never achieve what you never identified in the first place. You're also more likely to quit when you don't see immediate "results" that align with that static, inaccurate goal.

For example, let's say you want to lose twenty-five pounds because in your heyday you weighed twenty-five pounds less and looking back you looked freaking amazing—and you'd give anything to look like that again. Well, I hate to break it to you, but you could lose those twenty-five pounds and they could look like fifty on your more mature body. Maybe it makes you look sick and unhealthy. Or you could lose it and still wear the same pant size you do today, just a little looser. Or you could lose seventeen pounds and feel great but not allow yourself to feel amazing because, in your arbitrary mind, you didn't reach your goal of twenty-five. You could also lose it, be the same size you used to be, but not feel anything like you expected to feel. In fact, you'll probably feel exactly the same about your body as you do right now.

Why, you ask? Because that arbitrary number means nothing. It should never have been the goal in the first place. What you *should* figure out is this: how do I want to *feel* in that outfit I've always wanted to wear? How do I want to feel when I walk into a room? When I go on a date? When I walk up a flight of stairs? When I play with my kids? When I dance the night away? When I go for a hike?

These are your "whys." They are your real reasons for wanting to make a change to your health and fitness. And when you identify what really matters to *you*—and start using daydreaming to imagine those moments—you will be motivated to show up for yourself, one day at a time.

Start with daydreaming. Imagine all the moments that matter most to you, think of how you'll look, how you'll feel, what you'll wear, and why you care. Then see that version of yourself every time you work out. Imagine yourself morphing into that "You 2.0" with each workout, each glass of water, and every choice that supports your I AM Statements.

Next, you must align your mindset with your effort if you want to get to those new desired outcomes. Use Mental Tennis, I AM Statements, and Power Mottos to tell yourself every day how you want to feel and to remind yourself who you're becoming. They will begin to work their magic to encourage you to be consistent, regardless of whether you see measurable results right away or not. And now that your goals are aligned with what really matters—how you want to feel and the things you want to do in your new fit and healthy life—you'll begin seeing that needle shift much faster than pounds on a scale or body fat percentages. You'll start noticing that you do feel more energetic, that you feel more confident when you walk into a room, and so on. That positive reinforcement, combined with your new positive inner dialogue, will keep you on the path of consistency as a way of life and daily habit.

Power Mottos: Here are some examples…

- "I know my work is paying off even if I don't see it right away."
- "I can do it, I am strong."
- "My body is changing for the better every day. I am transforming and loving how I feel!"

What's the Mindset Shift I Need to Make Health a Lifestyle, Not a Punishment?

Again, it all comes down to what you tell yourself. If you keep saying, "I hate eating healthy and working out," then of course it's going to feel like punishment. But when you use daydreaming to picture yourself living in a healthy body that you love, everything shifts. It stops being a chore or a means to an end—and becomes part of a luxurious lifestyle.

When you feel fit and energized, you can say yes to all the fun spontaneous things you want to do—without overthinking it. That's the real reward: being able to do what you want, when you want, and truly enjoying your body.

At that point, working out isn't something you have to do, it's something you want to do (most days). It becomes a meaningful part of a fulfilling, well-rounded life. It's a way to care for and honor your body so it can support you in living a long vibrant life.

I stopped seeing food as the enemy when I went to Italy and honestly, it rocked my world. I began to view it the way Italians do, as a source of pure pleasure, passion, and love. That mindset shift changed everything. It made me want to eat meals made with beautiful fresh ingredients and enjoy the process of cooking them for my family. Food became something to savor and celebrate, not something to restrict or fear. And that naturally started to detox me from the pull of processed, fast, and packaged food. Without forcing it, I found myself choosing to cook because I genuinely started to love it. Now, it is one of my personal passions;; one day I'd love to attend culinary school or open a Bread & Breakfast in Italy. I've come a long way!

I work out to clear my head, to feel that endorphin high, and to sleep well at night. All of that became part of a deeper mental lifestyle shift for me. I stopped seeing exercise as a punishment or something I had to do to fix what was "wrong" with me and started seeing it as part of the beautiful intentional life I wanted to live.

Love Mindset

How to Improve All Your Relationships (and Manifest Love!)

Chapter 31

How Do I Manifest Love?

How to Change Your Mindset to Attract Healthy Love

Last January, I sat down with my journal and wrote a six-page life plan story. In it, I detailed the "must-have" qualities, characteristics, and values of the man I wanted to manifest into my life and the type of relationship I wanted. I poured my heart into describing not just who he was but how our love would feel, the kind of connection I dreamed of experiencing, how he'd treat me, what our dynamic together would be like, and so on.

Fast forward five months later to our first date…and we've been together ever since. I tell him all the time, "I wrote you into existence!" because he is truly everything I asked for and more.

This experience reaffirmed one of the foundational truths I teach: When you get crystal clear about what you want and refuse to settle for anything less than you deserve, the Universe will deliver.

But here's the catch—the Universe delivers only when you're ready to receive it. Before we met, I spent years doing the personal work to heal and grow, preparing myself to show up fully for the kind of love I dreamed of manifesting. He did the same work on himself before we met, and that's why it works. If you're ready to manifest your dream relationship, here is my proven five-step process. I've been teaching this process to clients for nearly a decade, and it's helped them manifest soulmates, partners, marriages, and even families. If it worked for us, it could work for you too!

I have a philosophy that applies to just about everything in life you'd like to manifest or achieve. I call it "Get ready to be ready." Here's how you can start getting ready, starting today to attract the love you desire and deserve.

Manifesting love isn't about *searching* for your "soulmate" or *chasing* after love; it's about preparing yourself to receive the kind of love and relationship you truly desire. I'm sure you've heard the saying "become the love you seek to attract." That's exactly what we are talking about.

You can't manifest your ideal partner until you've done the work to *become* an ideal partner.

This starts with being honest with yourself and identifying areas you need to work on—now, while you're single. Reflect on feedback from past relationships, as there's often valuable insight in how others have perceived you. This doesn't mean accepting all criticism as truth, but it's important to approach it with an open mind and ask yourself tough questions.

For example: *Could there be truth in what they said about me? Am I too impatient? Do I become mean or dismissive when communicating? Do I focus on faults instead of appreciating and building up my partner?*

Step 1: Heal Yourself, Know Yourself

The first and most critical step is doing the inner work. If you're holding onto unresolved pain or are stuck in negative relationship patterns, you're not yet ready to attract healthy, lasting love.

Personal Work ✍

Get your journal and answer these key questions:

- What went wrong in past relationships?
- What was *my part* in their demise?
- What patterns need to change?
- What signal have I been sending that attracts the wrong kind of partner?
- What are my emotional needs, triggers, and boundaries?
- What type of love do I need and want?
- What are some ways I like to have love expressed or shown to me?
- What type of partner have I been in the past?
- How am I going to evolve to become a better one in the future?
- What's my love language, how do I feel when my partner speaks it, and how do I feel when they don't?
- What's my attachment style, and how can I work on healing it?
- How can I improve my communication to foster understanding and connection?
- Do I know how to create a "safe space" for vulnerability? Have I listened to my intuition in the past or ignored red flags?
- What will I do differently this time?

- What do I need to change about myself?
- Do I love myself?
- Do I respect myself?
- Do I show up for myself?
- What dating behaviors have I exhibited in the past that I can change so I can get a different result?

This level of self-awareness is the foundation of a strong relationship and is critical to creating a healthy and healed *you*. When you take the time to know yourself, heal, and grow, you create the space to attract a partner who has done the same.

Suggested books that helped me get ready for love:

- *The Five Love Languages* by Gary Chapman
- *Attached* by Amir Levine and Rachel Heller
- *Secure Love* by Julie Menanno (Follow Julie @ thesecurerelationship.) This book was an absolute game-changer for me!

Step 2: Write Down What You Want

Clarity is the key to getting what you want. My six-page journal entry in January 2024 led to manifesting my love just five months later. Here are some of the questions I asked myself while writing about my dream relationship. They helped me truly see and feel what it would be like to be in a loving, happy, and healed relationship.

Note: Don't write down physical traits. Listen, if you've been going after "your type" all these years and it hasn't worked, it doesn't take a genius to recognize that maybe "your type" isn't the right kind of partner for you. This time around, focus on what genuinely matters—qualities that lead to healthy and fulfilling relationships—not the surface stuff that's gotten you into bad or toxic relationships in the past.

I definitely had a type, and I'd casually dated versions of that type for years before meeting my person. Every one of those relationships was *horrible* for me. Those guys were my worst possible match. When I finally sat down to write my list, I knew the love I wanted probably wouldn't come in the package I was used to chasing. That's why, at the top of my list, I wrote: "This is how you'll recognize him when you meet him, by who he is as a man, not by that instant chemical attraction you've always relied on."

Dive into the emotional depth of your connection and who the person is on a deeper level. For example, instead of writing, "I want someone funny," say, "I want someone who can make me laugh when I need it most and who sees humor as a way to connect."

Personal Work

Grab your journal and write down a detailed description of the person you want to attract. Write in full sentences: This helps you *see* and *feel* what it would be like to have that person in your life.

- Describe your ideal mate as a person: What are their values, personality, and qualities?
- What makes you feel loved, appreciated, and seen?
- How do you want to feel and be treated in the relationship?
- How will they show up for you, and how will you show up for them?

- How will you be as a couple? What will that dynamic be like?
- What's most important to you in a partner?
- What are your top-ten "must haves"? (Note: These should not be surface level.)

Step 3: Use Daydreaming

Visualization is a powerful tool for manifesting love and the more time you spend daydreaming about your ideal relationship and how it will *feel*, the faster you'll draw it to you. Close your eyes and really try to see your future life, one where you are happy, adored, heard, seen, appreciated, and having fun!

- How is your partner expressing love through their actions? Write out a specific scenario.
- How do they make you feel safe, secure, seen, and appreciated? Write specific things you imagine them doing to make you feel this way.
- What does it feel like to laugh, have fun, and enjoy each other's company? Write specific ways you enjoy life together.
- What does it feel like to have someone you can grow and experience life with? Write down the ways you want to grow together and things you'd like to do together.
- What does your daily life look like?
- How do you interact with each other? With your friends and family?
- How do you lift each other up and express yourselves?
- How do you treat them that is different from how you've treated past partners?

- How do you make each other better, stronger, and more motivated to both be your best?
- How have you learned to speak their love language and to give them what they need?
- How do you resolve conflict that's different from anything you've experienced in the past?

By focusing your energy on the feeling of being in your dream relationship, you align yourself with its frequency.

Step 4: Make a Love #Futureboard

Take your vision to the next level by creating a #Futureboard for love. (If you're serious about manifesting love, my book *#Futureboards* walks you through exactly how to do it.) Pinterest is one of the best tools for this. Look for images that reflect the kind of connection you want, the way you want to feel in a relationship, and the experiences you want to share. When you're searching, try phrases like "couple" plus the activity or feeling you want—like "couple cooking together photography" or "couple laughing on a beach photography." This step helps bring your vision to life and keeps it front and center every day.

Step 5: Change Your Mindset

The final step is aligning your thoughts and words with the relationship you're manifesting. Your mindset sets the tone for what you attract, so use your tools to reinforce your readiness and worthiness for love.

My Favorite Love Power Mottos

- "I am worthy and deserving of love."

- "I am loved."
- "I am cherished."
- "I am open and ready to receive love."
- "I am ready for a healthy, happy, and lasting love."
- "I know my value, my worth, and will never settle for less than I deserve; true love is on its way to me."
- "I am working on myself, so I'll be ready when my love shows up."
- "Somewhere out there, my love is preparing for me just as I am preparing for them."
- "I will know my love by how safe, secure, and cherished I feel."

Repeat these daily, and use them to replace any negative or limiting beliefs you have about love.

Pro Tip

Healthy love feels different from toxic love. It's a slow burn, not the instant chemical reaction we were falsely taught to believe is love. When you focus on attracting a healthy, healed, and connected love, be prepared for it to look a little different from what you're used to. It's a slow burn, not an instant bonfire.

Though we've been together since our first date, we built our relationship on friendship first, taking the time to let our feelings grow organically. We invested in truly getting to know each other and trusted that our feelings would deepen with each interaction—and they have. So, when you meet someone who embodies the qualities you are looking for but maybe doesn't have that instant spark, give it time to build a slow burn. Don't decide too early on, because feelings can grow and deepen with time invested.

I heard someone say once, and it couldn't be more accurate…

"Women are always seeking fireworks when what we really want is a fireplace."

Work on healing, self-discovery, and growth. As you do, you'll naturally attract someone who mirrors the love, energy, and values you've cultivated within yourself. When I met my love, I realized the Universe had been waiting for me to be ready; once I'd done my work, he appeared.

Work on you. Heal you. When you're genuinely ready, love will manifest in ways that will feel nothing short of magical.

Chapter 32

How Do I Stop People-Pleasing and Set Boundaries?

How to Break Unhealthy Relationship Patterns

If you've found yourself in the same kinds of relationships throughout your life, there's likely a pattern we can identify and shift, so you can start attracting a different type of person and dynamic into your life. This isn't just about romantic relationships—it shows up in friendships, acquaintances, and even with bosses and coworkers. The energy we put out is powerful. It draws in people who respond to it in very specific ways.

For example, if you're a people pleaser, you've probably noticed a pattern in your closest relationships. Whether it's with a parent, sibling, partner, friend, coworker, or boss—chances are, many of them have played a similar role. They've tended to be dominant, while you've often taken a more passive or accommodating role. They likely made most of the decisions that affected you, told you what they wanted, and you went along with it to "keep the peace."

You might've asked yourself, why do I always end up in relationships where the people closest to me are dominant, bossy, or even straight-up bullies? How does this keep happening? Why can't I ever have a kind thoughtful people pleaser as *my* best friend, partner, or boss?

It might feel like one of life's great mysteries, but it's unsurprising. Dominant people are drawn to people pleasers. They need that softer, more submissive energy around them to keep feeling in control or "alpha." And without even realizing it, people pleasers often feel more comfortable with someone telling them what to do or how to be, because deep down, they may not fully trust themselves to make the "right" choices. Hence, the cycle continues repeating.

I've worked with hundreds of clients over the years who've identified as people pleasers, and through our work, they've come to realize how much that behavior has held them back. From their perspective, they're coming from a good place. They just want to make the people around them happy. They want to avoid conflict, keep the peace, and diffuse tension. A lot of them learned early on that if they stayed agreeable and kept their opinions to themselves, the more volatile person in their life would calm down.

For many, this started as a survival instinct. It was a coping mechanism that helped them navigate tough or even scary situations in childhood. Maybe it meant hiding from an angry parent or saying what that parent wanted to hear just to avoid a blowup. But over time, what started as a way to survive turned into a pattern that kept attracting the same "parent-like" personalities into their adult lives.

They might end up in relationships with partners who treat them the way that dominant parent did or working for a boss who carries that same energy. No matter what they try, it feels like they can't stop emitting the signal that keeps pulling these people in. And the longer that pattern continues, the more muted they become—burying their voice, their opinions, their wants and needs. Eventually, they don't even know who they are without those dominant relationships.

Client Example: I once had a client who was the "submissive twin" in her relationship with her dominant twin sister. This is a fairly common twin dynamic. As a mom of identical twin daughters, I know this firsthand, and I'm always working with them to keep their relationship as balanced as possible.

From the very beginning, this client had taken on the role of being the "passive one." Over time, that allowed her twin to take over in ways that dismissed her wants, minimized her voice, and pushed her aside. Her twin would put her down, ignore what she needed, and essentially steamroll her in most situations.

As we worked together to help her find her voice and identify what she truly wanted—not just in specific situations, but in her life as a whole—she began to realize it wasn't just her sister who treated her this way. The same pattern showed up in most of her closest relationships. I explained that these patterns usually get set from the very first interaction. That early energy creates the tone of the relationship. One person steps into the role of being in charge, and the other quietly agrees to go along with it. It's like one says, "I'll wear the pants," and the other says, "Great, those pants look amazing on you!"

To break that cycle and start creating boundaries, we first had to change her beliefs about herself. We needed to rebuild her in the places where those relationships had worn her down. So, we started with I AM Statements. Every day, she repeated things like "I am heard." "I am seen." "I am valued." "I am appreciated." "I am understood." "I am smart." "I am capable."

Then we added a few Power Mottos to help strengthen her voice, instincts, and boundaries. Things like "I am important. My voice and opinions matter." "I need to tell people how I feel in order to be heard." "If I don't like something, it's okay to say something." "People will still love me even if I share my opinions, thoughts, and ideas." "I don't always need to do what other people want just to be liked." "I listen to my instincts and trust my intuition. I trust myself to make good decisions and to know what I want."

Each week we worked on real-life ways she could begin speaking up and letting her voice be heard. She practiced at work, in her relationship, and eventually with her twin. At first, it was terrifying. This was a version of her the people around her had never seen before. They weren't expecting it. But I showed her how to have those conversations in a way that didn't trigger defensiveness. It's the same way I've been teaching you in this book.

And something amazing happened. Each time she spoke up, she got a new and unexpected reaction—a better one than she'd anticipated. She couldn't believe it. I reminded her that if she'd never said anything before, if she'd never once indicated that something bothered her, the people in her life had no way of knowing it did. Now they knew, and now they could modify their behavior to be more accommodating and empathetic. Sometimes it really is that simple.

People aren't mind readers. Letting them know what you think, in a way that doesn't accuse or blame, can be all it takes to start shifting the relationship in a positive direction.

Other times, it becomes clear that the relationship is toxic or unhealthy, because the other person only wants people they can control. And in those cases, it's time to walk away.

Luckily, she's been able to make an incredible transformation. The people in her life have respected her new boundaries and adapted, and now she feels comfortable using her voice and speaking up. She's able to clearly express herself and speak up when they've been crossed.

The energy we put out into the world—the signal that pulls people into our orbit—is a direct reflection of our self-beliefs. When we can identify what those beliefs are, we can change them and thereby change the signal. If your belief sounds like, "Why should I tell anyone what I think or how I feel? They won't care anyway," then you'll keep attracting people who confirm that belief: people who don't care. People who don't listen. It becomes a self-fulfilling prophecy that keeps repeating.

We do that by using I AM Statements and Power Mottos as part of our daily offensive mindset practice. We say things like: "My voice matters. My thoughts and opinions matter." "People want to hear what I have to say." "I am heard, respected, and understood by the people in my life." These tools start building our confidence. They help us find our voice, help us pause in the moment to check in with what we want and what we think, and they give us the courage to say it out loud. That starts to shift our energy. And once our energy changes, we begin attracting people who respect us, who care about what we have to say, and who value our thoughts and opinions.

Eventually we won't always need to set verbal boundaries, because people can sense them and have a new level of respect for us, one that matches our newly adjusted signal. But when a boundary does need to be communicated, we now have the confidence to say it clearly and follow through without guilt.

Chapter 33

Can I Change My Relationship Without Changing My Partner?

How Changing Your Mindset Can Improve Your Relationship

IRL Example: You're married or in a long-term relationship with someone you want to stay with, but you're going through a difficult time, or you're just not completely satisfied with how things are. Maybe you've gotten into a rut. Maybe you feel unseen or underappreciated. Maybe the romance has taken an unexpected indefinite hiatus.

Don't you hate it when your relationship slips into that negative pattern of nagging, snapping at each other, and walking around with tension so thick you could cut it with a fork? It's the worst. And when that happens, it can feel like things are out of your control—like you're just waiting for something to magically turn the vibe around.

But there is something you can do that can completely reset the energy in your relationship. I call it "bees and honey," and you already know where I'm going with this.

Let's start with nagging. It's one of the most common complaints in almost every relationship. Ladies, we hate doing it just as much as our partner hates hearing it, right? Nagging builds ongoing tension and resentment. It makes us feel unheard and makes our partner feel unappreciated. You've been learning throughout this book that the energy we put out is the same energy that is reflected back to us. If we are constantly nagging—complaining, venting, or feeling like we're talking to a wall—what we'll get in return is resistance, defensiveness, more frustration, and even less effort.

Most people respond better to encouragement and kindness than they do to criticism. That means the best way to get your partner to help more around the house, be more thoughtful, or give you more attention is by noticing and praising the efforts they are making.

If you only focus on what they're not doing, you'll keep seeing more of what you *don't* want. But when you focus on the good—what they are doing *right*—you'll start seeing more of that instead.

IRL Example: If you've been asking your partner every day to take out the trash and are getting more annoyed each time they forget, and then on the one day they finally do, you hit them with, "Well, it's about time." That's not going to help. That just reinforces the negative cycle. They're probably thinking, "Why bother? My partner is never happy anyway."

Instead, notice it in the moment. Say thank you. Give a smile, a hug, a kiss. Show appreciation the same way you did when you first started dating. Reward the behavior you want to see more of.

Now, I get it, this might sound overly simple—but it works. Is it fair that you are the one making the shift, especially if they're the one who's been checked out or "needs to change?" No, it's not. But if what you've been doing hasn't been working and the relationship feels like it's falling apart, isn't it worth trying something different?

Changing your energy is the one thing you have the most control over. You can't control them or the energy they bring into the relationship, but you can choose to shift yours. And by doing that, you influence the entire vibe between you.

In my experience, positive reinforcement is the fastest and most effective way to change the energy in your relationship. It takes the tension down and helps you stop walking on eggshells. Your partner wants to feel appreciated too. When they don't feel seen or valued, they tend to pull away or lash out. But when they see that their efforts are making a difference, they usually want to keep showing up.

Try it Out for Yourself

Try this out for one week and just see what happens. You'll usually feel a shift in energy within a few days, but if things have been tense for a while, it might take a little longer. This is a simple experiment to see how much power you have in controlling your energy and how that energy impacts your partner and the relationship. If you really want things to improve, sometimes you need to be the one to lead by example.

- Start with something small. Ask your partner kindly, with a calm tone, to do something specific within a certain time. For example, "Hey babe, do you mind taking out the trash before work?" Add a smile, maybe a kiss or hug. You're modeling the kind of energy you want in return. This isn't about being fake or sucking up—it's about getting back to a kind and respectful way of communicating.

- If they do it, send a thank-you text or a voice note that expresses how much you appreciate them. Let them know you noticed. That's probably what you did when you first started dating.
- If they forgot, don't say a word about it when they get home. Still show love and affection. If they remember on their own and do it before the day ends, notice it. Say thank you. Let them see that follow-through matters to you and is appreciated.
- If they don't do it at all, ask again the next day with the same kind tone. No sarcasm. No attitude. Just repeat the process.
- Don't take over and do the task yourself. Give them the chance to show up.

That's a simplistic example, but you can apply this approach to anything. Keep it simple and specific. Don't pile on ten things at once. You're experimenting here to see what works best for your relationship. The goal is to build a new communication pattern based on kindness, appreciation, and love—and to always lead by example.

Give freely the love you wish to receive. Treat your partner how you want to be treated.

When your partner starts to feel seen and appreciated, you'll start seeing a shift in how they show up for you. It might take time. Trust must be rebuilt, especially if there has been long-term tension. In the beginning, they might still be expecting the old version of you to quickly reemerge—ready to fight or to criticize—but when you meet them with calm loving energy, it diffuses the tension. And when you show real happiness and appreciation when they follow through or make an effort, they will want to keep getting this positive response from you.

Soon, the way you are treating them will begin to shift the way they treat you. That's how you reset the energy in your relationship.

If your mate used to be thoughtful, kind, or affectionate, this can help reactivate these qualities in them. If they never were, well, that's a different story.

This is simply applying the law of attraction to your relationship in a real, practical way. And it really works. Once you get past the initial ego trip of feeling like you're the one making the effort, the joy of seeing measurable change will make it more than worth it.

Remember to reinforce positive effort with verbal affirmations. Tell them how much you appreciate them, see them, and love them. And stop verbalizing all the things you don't like, focus on what you want to see more of instead. That doesn't mean you don't tell someone when they are doing something you don't like, it just means you stop nagging them about it and find a new and healthier way to communicate and connect with them. Because as we know, what you focus on expands. Focus on the good.

What If My Partner Isn't Growing or Interested in Doing Mindset Work?

This is a question I get a lot, and like always, I'm not going to sugarcoat my answer.

When you do deep personal growth work, you transform. That's the whole point, right? But when you start making real changes in your mindset, in how you think, and in how you show up, and you begin getting clear on what you want, it can create a visible and undeniable divide between you and a partner who isn't willing to grow.

I always tell my clients, this work doesn't create the divide—it reveals it. It brings to the surface and highlights issues that have been there all along. In an ideal world, you grow together. But when one person is willing to do the work and the other isn't, it will eventually bring those differences to the surface.

By doing this work, you'll build confidence. You'll start becoming the version of yourself you've always wanted to be. You'll get clear on what you want in every area of your life and have the tools to go after it. You'll know how to communicate your needs, trust your decisions, and stand in your worth. And because of that, you'll expect the people in your life to treat you with the love and respect you deserve.

If you've been in a relationship that you've known for a while isn't good for you, this work can help you walk away from what's no longer serving you and start attracting what is.

On the other hand, if you're in the right relationship, your partner will appreciate the changes you're making. They'll most likely become curious about what's helping you grow. They'll see that the work is making you a better, happier version of yourself, and they'll be happy for you. They might not fully understand what you're doing, but they'll support it because they love and support *you.*

They don't need to do the work with you for the relationship to grow. They simply need to respect your journey and support the fact that this matters to you.

For example, my love is a very faith-based and religious person. For him, God is the center of his beliefs and his grounding force. For me, the Universe is my grounding force, and I'm not religious. But because we fully love and respect each other, we also love and respect each other's beliefs and how we choose to practice them.

We're both completely supportive of one another. I've gone to church with him, and he's adopted many of my beliefs about mindset and manifesting. We don't have to be doing the exact same work or believe the exact same things to have a deep, loving, and respectful relationship. What matters is that we support each other in the ways that are meaningful to each of us.

Chapter 34

Relationship Q&A

How Do I Stop Settling for Less Than I Deserve?

I'd challenge you on this—do you really know what you deserve? Hopefully you do now, after doing the work in this book. But before that, if you're honest, you probably didn't. And because you weren't clear in the past about what you deserved or how you wanted to be treated, you couldn't attract it. That signal was never sent—which is exactly why it never showed up.

If you didn't believe you were worthy of love, or if you believed all men or women would cheat or mistreat you, then that's what kept showing up. Your beliefs were sending that signal, *please send me a cheater!* Now that you've done the work, you can finally send a different signal and attract someone who'd never cheat on you.

In the past you probably said, "I don't want a partner who cheats." Or you filled in the blank with all the things you *didn't* want. The problem is that the mind focuses on the subject of that sentence, and the Universe responds to that subject. So, you kept attracting partners who cheated because that was the energy and focus you were putting out. To put it bluntly, knowing what you don't want in a relationship is exactly why you keep manifesting what you don't want. That's why the *Think It* tools are so powerful. Now, you know how to shift your focus and energy toward what you do want instead.

It's like going to a restaurant and telling the waiter you don't want steak. They'll probably say, "Okay cool, but what do you want *instead*?" If you can't give them an answer and just keep saying you don't want steak, eventually they're going to walk away shaking their head, and you'll never get that beautiful plate of Dover sole. Because you never asked for Dover sole. That order was never sent.

This book has taught you how to send the right order. How to focus on what you want instead of what you don't. And now you have a real shot at getting exactly what you asked for or something even better.

Start with your I AM Statements and Power Mottos to build your beliefs about who you are and what you deserve. This will help you recognize when someone doesn't meet those standards, and you'll be able to walk away with confidence, knowing they aren't right for you. You'll know with certainty (if you practice this work) that the right one is still out there and will come into your life when you're ready.

Now, you'll truly know your value and your worth, and anything less won't even be appealing. You'll stop finding yourself in relationships where you're the only one giving, because you'll naturally be drawn to someone who gives just as freely.

Is There Something Wrong with Me If I'm Still Single?

No! Being single can be a beautiful thing. Trust me, I was intentionally single for seventeen years before meeting my guy a year ago. It was such a valuable time for me to focus on myself, my children, my career, and becoming the woman I wanted to be. And remember, the more you fight against it, the more you push love away.

If you're tired of being single, the best thing you can do to attract healthy love is to change your beliefs—about yourself, about relationships, and about men, women, or partners. That's where the signal shifts. That's what starts bringing love to you instead of pushing it away.

When you love yourself and love your life exactly as it is right now, that energy brings all kinds of love, joy, and happiness into your life. That's something you have control over. When you stop focusing on not having love and start focusing on all the love you already do have, that's when it shows up. So use your tools. They work.

Why Is It So Hard for Me to Believe Someone Could Truly Love Me for Me?

Because that has been your belief, and that's why you've manifested it in the past. Now it's time to remove that belief using Mental Tennis, I AM Statements, and Power Mottos until you fully believe that there is absolutely someone out there who will love and adore every part of you. All the things past partners rejected, called "too much," or didn't value—the right partner will see those parts of you as beautiful. They'll love and appreciate all of you.

What If I've Never Seen the Kind of Relationship I Want—How Do I Believe It's Possible?

That's why it's so important to write out that detailed list of what your ideal love, partner, and relationship looks like to you, just like the "Personal Work" assignment in chapter 31. You must identify all those elements and then practice daydreaming about your ideal relationship as often as possible. Let it fill you with excitement, anticipation, and hope.

Fill up your Pinterest love #Futureboard so you can visually see what that kind of relationship looks like. Then use your Power Mottos and I AM Statements to build a solid unwavering belief that this kind of love not only exists but is already making its way to you.

Is It Too Late in Life for Me to Find Love?

God, no! My beautiful lifelong mentor Duffie Bart found love at age seventy-eight, and fourteen years later they are still the cutest couple ever! My good friend Nancy Bruce found the love of her life, whom she married in her mid-fifties. I found my love at forty-nine; it's never too late.

Chapter 35

How Do I Use Think It to Parent More Intentionally?

How to Teach These Tools to Your Kids

Parenting is the most important job we will ever have in life and one we step into with no training, no experience, and no verified qualifications, yet it's the one with the highest stakes. I know firsthand how overwhelming and lonely that can feel, especially when you're trying to break generational cycles, raise emotionally healthy kids, and model a mindset you're still working on yourself.

I've always believed that as parents, our greatest résumé in life is our children. They're a reflection of us in every way. Yes, that's a heavy responsibility—and honestly, a little scary when you think about it—but it's true. We are their greatest teacher, whether we intend to be or not. So, I encourage you to embrace that role and teach them all the things you wish you'd known as a kid, a teen, or a young adult.

This isn't about being the perfect parent, it's about being intentional, present, and teaching through example. And if you're anything like I was as a single mom raising three kids, you've probably had moments when you reacted out of stress, frustration, or guilt...only to lie awake later wishing you'd handled it differently. We all want to raise confident, kind, emotionally strong kids, but how do we do that when most of the time we're just trying to make it through the day? We use our tools and teach them to our kids. We can show them how to recognize their thoughts, manage their emotions, and choose their point of focus. And the beautiful part is that kids pick this stuff up so quickly, especially when they see *us* doing it too.

I believe it's so important that we teach our kids how to manage their inner voice—how to talk to themselves in a kind, confident, and supportive way—just like we're learning to do for ourselves.

Here's how you can adapt the seven tools in this book to use as a powerful parenting tool, teaching them how to align their thoughts with the outcomes they want. How to build genuine self-confidence. How to build mental strength, toughness, and fortitude that will make them better equipped to handle adversity. How to protect their emotions and feelings from the meanness of other kids and so much more.

It's never too early to start, I started using these methods with my kids from infancy on. And it's never too late to start either, whatever age you are today, don't you wish someone had taught you these tools even a year ago? See, it's never too late. Imagine if you had learned how to silence your inner critic back in middle school. Or if, as a teenager, you knew how to build your confidence through positive I AM Statements. Now you can give that gift to your children.

Personal Example:

My son Kanen has always been a sensitive, kind, and deeply caring human. He never wants to disappoint anyone—especially the adults in his life like me, his teachers, or his coaches. He's a rule follower by nature, and when he was really little, especially after my divorce, he was prone to feeling anxious or nervous, mostly around change.

I realized early on that I needed to help him build confidence. To believe that he was capable of doing things for himself. I wanted him to know how to calm himself when he felt overwhelmed or unsure. And just as importantly, I wanted to teach him that advocating for yourself—asking questions or speaking up—isn't "being a problem" or "breaking the rules." It's actually a sign of his engagement and a desire to understand things more deeply.

The two of us have always shared a love of football, especially for the Oregon Ducks. Starting when Kanen was about six, I began taking him to games at Autzen Stadium. Afterward, we'd wait near the tunnel where the players walked off the field, and he'd hold out his little fist for a quick bump as they passed. His eyes were always full of admiration and big dreams.

I took those moments as golden opportunities to pour into his dreams. I'd ask him, "Can you imagine what it would feel like to be one of those players someday?" I encouraged him to talk to me about his wild little-kid fantasies of being a big football star. And then I'd flood him with I AM affirmations, telling him that he possessed the needed focus and determination to make it happen if he really wanted to. But in reality, he was the opposite. At that time, he was struggling with getting frustrated too easily and getting mad at himself when he didn't get something perfect right away. When that would happen, he'd want to quit. Especially if he was corrected or "coached" during the learning process.

But I knew that was a trait we needed to flip immediately, because left unchecked, it can hold someone back in every area of life. So, I began telling him he *was* already the things I wanted him to grow into or the characteristics I knew he needed to develop. Because we know this: kids form their self-beliefs early, and they get most of them from their parents. Knowing this, I was very intentional about what I told him "he was."

I'd say things like, "I love that when I show you a new way to do something, you pick it up right away. That's such an important skill, and I'm so proud you have it." And yes—I was saying things like this to a five-year-old. And I kept saying them until I didn't need to anymore…because eventually, *he* knew that's who he was. His coachability and adaptability became a cornerstone of his success in football. He became incredibly coachable—able to take feedback without spiraling and eager to improve. That mindset helped him stand out and rise as a leader on every team he played on.

In fact, when he was recently hired by the College Football Playoffs—one of only five interns selected out of over a thousand applicants—his new boss told him that part of what stood out in his interview was when she asked how he learns, and he'd responded, "I learn like a sponge and adapt like clay."

That one sentence says a lot about who he is.

Kanen's grown into a confident, emotionally intelligent, kind, and grounded young man. He's not afraid to take risks. He's a leader. He advocates for himself and others. And no, I'm not taking credit for who he is—but I *am* saying that I gave him the tools throughout his childhood to become the man he wanted to be. I taught him how to build himself up instead of tear himself down, and that gave him the confidence and trust in himself that he now carries into everything he does.

And that's just one example. I've done the same with my daughters, Mira and Izzy, throughout their lives. I've adapted my approach, my style, and communication to fit their unique personalities and learning styles. These tools have helped them build confidence in so many real-life ways: making new friends, learning to drive and passing their driver's tests, flying across the country solo, landing jobs, crushing interviews, and even launching their own businesses.

Tool 1: Snapping In—Teach Them How to Pay Attention to Their Thoughts

When you start parenting your kids using the *Think It* tools, talk to them about it. Let them know you've been learning something interesting from a book that taught you how powerful your thoughts are, and how you can train them like muscles at the gym to start creating cool new things in your life. Tell them you need help practicing and sticking to your new commitment. Be real with them. Say you're working hard not to speak negatively about yourself, other people, or your life—and instead, you're learning how to claim what you want and speak it into existence. Invite them to help keep you accountable. Give them permission to call you out if they hear you slip and let them be part of your mindset training. That alone teaches them so much. This conversation lays the groundwork for you to start coaching them using these tools.

Explain to them that learning how to notice their thoughts is the first step. Make it fun and interactive. Say, "You can ask me anytime, 'Hey Mama (or Dad), what are you thinking about right now?'" And you do the same for them. Throughout the day, casually ask, "Hey honey, what are you thinking about right now?"

Not only does this help them build awareness of their thoughts, but it also keeps the conversation open between you and encourages them to share what's going on in their little minds. And that's a powerful life skill; one most adults were never taught. Giving them the tools to express what you're thinking and feeling to someone else is such a gift.

From here, you can start to gently coach them using the other *Think It* tools. I've included examples that work for kids of all ages, but feel free to adapt to your parenting style and your kid's age and communication level.

Tool 2: Teach Them Mental Tennis in Real Time

Mental Tennis is the perfect tool to use *in the moment* to catch negative self-talk and flip it into something empowering. It's simple, effective, and easy for kids to grasp, especially when you model it in real time. See it. Stop it. Replace it.

Here's How to Do it:

When your child says something like, "I can't do that," you step in and say, "No, thank you, we don't talk like that, honey. What we say is what we believe, and if you want to hit that home run, I want to hear you say it. Tell me, 'I *can* hit home runs.'"

Now, depending on your kid's age or mood, they might roll their eyes, push back, or try to be funny. That's okay. Stick with it. Encourage them to say the positive version out loud. This is where they start learning that their words are powerful and that you're not just correcting them, you're teaching them how to get the results they *want.*

Explain that their words are like little predictions and if they want something different, they've got to change what they're saying (and thinking). That's why this matters so much and why you'll be making these types of corrections from now on. Because helping them get their words, thoughts, and actions aligned is how they'll start successfully getting the results they want. And how much do we love it when our kids win?

If your child says something negative, you can also respond with: "Well, we don't want that to happen, now do we? What *do* you want to happen instead?" Or: "What's the opposite of that?" That question alone helps them start thinking differently. And more importantly, it teaches them how to use this tool for themselves, which can alter the course of their life in the most positive way.

Tool 3: Pump Them Full of Positive I AM Statements

Tell your kids every single day that they *are* the things they want to be—or the qualities you're working to cultivate in them. Say things like, "Honey, you're so smart. I love how you always stick with things, even when they're hard." Or when they're heading out the door: "Hey, don't forget...you're smart, you're capable, you make friends easily, and people love being around you!"

Customize these I AM Statements to your child's fears, doubts, or insecurities, so they're constantly hearing affirmations that reflect who they want to become and remove those negative thoughts, preventing them from becoming concreate negative beliefs. Confidence is built through repetition and specifics, so point out the moments they show courage or follow-through. Call out how they handled something well. Praise them every time they catch a negative thought and flip it into something positive.

And most importantly—model this by saying your own I AM statements out loud around them.

For example: I've always made a point to speak positively about my body and appearance around my girls, long before I believed it myself. From the time they were babies, if they saw me getting dressed or doing my makeup, I'd say things like, "Oh, I feel so good in this outfit. This looks great on me, doesn't it, girls?" That might sound conceited to some, but it wasn't about ego. It was about breaking a generational cycle of the women in my family hating their bodies. It was about my determination to not pass on the same self-hatred to my daughters. I was not about to let them inherit the nasty bitch who lived in my head for most of my life. Instead, I wanted to normalize feeling confident, loving your body, and talking kindly to yourself.

I also told them every single day that they were beautiful—not just because I believe it's true, but because I wanted that message to come from inside their home. I never wanted them out in the world chasing that validation from the wrong people. And I wanted them to believe it. So, I taught them to say it to themselves too.

We did this with everything, not just appearance.

If they were trying a new activity at school or preparing for a test, I'd tell them they were capable, ready, and able to crush it. I'd remind them of specific things they'd done before to prove it. "Remember when you gave that presentation and your teacher said it was one of the best in class?" or "You finished that whole book in just a few days, that's how focused you can be. You've already proven that if you want something, you can make it happen, so let's do it again for this."

Kids learn best from examples and from being shown how to do something differently in the moment. When you anchor their strengths to real-life proof, you help them build genuine confidence based on their own experience.

Tool 4: Power Mottos

Teach your kids how to create a Power Motto for the things they worry about most—the fears, insecurities, or thoughts they tend to obsess over. These mottos help them reframe their thinking and start building empowering new beliefs.

Start by asking them how they want to feel *instead*. If your child is shy or nervous about making new friends, ask, "Would you like to feel confident? Friendly? Like someone everyone wants to talk to?" Get them to describe the version of themselves they want to become. Then, help them turn that into a Power Motto. Something like:

"I am friendly and kind. I make friends easily and everyone loves me!"

Say it with them, repeat it often, especially when those worries come up. The more they hear it, the more they'll begin to believe it. And the more they believe it, the more they'll start to *be* it.

Tool 5: Encourage their Childhood Daydreams

I know this can be hard as a parent because we tend to bring all our baggage to their dreams. We tend to tarnish their childlike optimism and imagination with our knowledge of "how the world works." But what if you've been wrong about how it works? What if the world was responding to your thoughts, beliefs, energy, and actions? Would things have gone differently in the past if you knew then what you're practicing now? The answer is yes, it probably would have. That's not to make us regret the past or feel guilt or frustration about it. It's just pointing out that maybe our experiences with getting the desires of our heart (or not) were affected by some factors we now know how to change.

I had a client recently whose eleven-year-old son wants to become a Broadway star. "How can I encourage such an insane and unrealistic goal for him?" she asked me. "Very few actors ever make it on Broadway. I don't want him to be disappointed." I get it. That's our natural reaction to our child's big dreams: *"But what if they get disappointed?"*

To that I say (and did say to her), *so what if he gets disappointed!* Who cares? In life, there will be plenty of disappointments. Learning how to adapt to and grow from adversity is what will make him great at anything he chooses to do. Shielding him from it will do the opposite. If he thinks *you* don't believe he can do it, he'll be less likely to go after what he wants—in acting or anything else—for the rest of his life.

And if there's even a one-percent chance that he makes the big stage, isn't that worth the risk of disappointment? Not to mention all the other opportunities that will come just by pursuing the dream. It could pay for his education—not a bad outcome. It'll put him in a small circle of elite individuals he'd never have access to otherwise. It could open doors to other amazing career paths. My son was never a "big football star," but if hadn't played football at the level he did, there's no way he would've gotten the opportunity at the CFP. The connections he made through football will impact the rest of his life in countless incredible ways.

The other day, I met a twenty-year-old guy in the green room at *AM Northwest*, Portland's ABC morning show, where I'm a regular contributor. He was also a guest on that morning's show, there to talk about how he'd designed a LEGO version of Cinque Terre, Italy. LEGO had chosen his creation to be turned into a kit that would be sold worldwide, and he'd earn royalties from it. His proud parents were there too, and I couldn't help but silently thank them for not shutting down their kid's dream when he was probably eleven or twelve, talking about how he wanted to create LEGO kits.

Encourage those dreams, parents. You have nothing to lose. They're incredible opportunities to teach your child valuable life lessons, ones they might not learn any other way.

Tool 6: The Energy Bubble

This is a fun one to teach your kids. Walk them through the visuals and adapt the language to match their age and whatever situation they're dealing with. Maybe they're struggling with someone at school—this tool helps them learn how *not* to let other people's actions or words affect who they are. It teaches them to separate what others think or say from what they *know* about themselves. It helps disable the power others can have over their self-worth, identity, and personal beliefs.

My Parenting Ethos

I thought I'd leave you with my parenting ethos. These were "rules" I put in place for myself after my divorce, when my children were very young, to help me remember how to show up as the mama I wanted to be, even on the impossibly hard days.

I wanted to be a different kind of mother than I had. I wanted to be present, loving, and kind. I wanted to enjoy being their mama, and having these reminders helped me show up more consistently in that energy. They helped ensure that I wouldn't become my mother. That my children would have a different kind of childhood.

I was far from perfect, and it didn't always work, but looking back over the last seventeen years, I can honestly say I followed these rules most of the time—and they made me a better, more present parent. I'm proud of the memories we made, the big belly laughs, and the bond we formed, regardless of how hard life was at the time or what I was personally going through.

I hope these help you to remember that it will all be over in the blink of an eye. How can you make each day a memory?

Parents—remember to *breathe.*

Remember to walk into the other room and talk yourself off the ledge before yelling at your kids when they're being annoying, not listening, or disobeying. Try to hold your tongue in those moments, rather than say something you can't take back—words can seriously damage your kids, negatively shaping their identity, and hurt your bond.

Remember to tell them how smart, beautiful, brilliant, creative, interesting, and talented they are. And tell them how much you love them. EVERY. SINGLE. DAY.

Remember to get down on the floor to play with them, the laundry can wait.

Swing next to them on the swings instead of standing around scrolling on your phone.

Teach them things. Teach them *everything.* Explain the world to them. Prepare them for life, for new experiences. Teach them what to expect in various situations. Show them life. Teach them how to live it. Start young. Show them how things work, let them try with you. Don't do everything for them, show them how to do it for themselves. This builds their confidence and prepares them for life.

Remember to laugh out loud when they say or do something funny or silly and watch their face light up.

Just load them in the car and drive to that beach like you've been talking about. Even if it's going to be a long messy day. Or put that vacation on a credit card, because when will you get this time again? Or do the thing they've been wanting to do and do it *with them*. Spontaneous memories are often the best. They don't need to be perfect or even pretty—just *do them.*

Light up, smile with your eyes and soul, every time they walk in a room.

Remember to smell and kiss the top of their head, as often as you can get away with it.

Hug them at least once a day, even when they're grumpy teenagers. I've branded these hugs "food for the soul," and told my kids they are non-negotiable, because our soul needs to eat too.

Remember that one day, you'll even want the hard days *back.*

Because before you know it, all those busy, rushing, annoying days are gone—and you'll wish you'd paused to make them memories. I always had the goal of capturing a moment each day that I could remember. Of course that didn't always work, but parenting with that philosophy helped me, *try.*

Life is beautiful, and being a parent is the greatest gift imaginable.

Enjoy it all.

Epilogue

The #ThinkITChallenge

Join My Free, Twenty-One-Day Mental Fitness Challenge

Twenty-One Days. Five Minutes a Day. A Whole New Mindset.

Now it's your turn to train your thinking to get everything you want. You've done the reading, now let's do the rewiring! It's time to actually practice what you've learned so you can start seeing the real-life results you deserve.

The power is in the *practice.*

So go to https://www.sarahcentrella.com/thinkitchallenge right now and join my free **Twenty-One-Day Mental Fitness Challenge.** This is how you turn the tools in this book into real positive momentum in *your life*.

Every morning for twenty-one days, you'll get a short email challenge that helps you apply a specific mindset tool to a specific area of your life. It's simple, powerful, and designed to keep you accountable while you build real lasting mental habits.

To get the most out of this book—and to stay connected to a community of people doing the work with you—join the private **Think It Challenge Facebook group** (www.facebook.com/groups/thinkitchallenge) when you sign up. I'll be checking in there with bonus coaching and support to keep you moving forward.

I can't wait to hear your thoughts, wins, breakthroughs, and feedback. Share with me on Instagram by tagging @sarahcentrella and using the hashtag **#ThinkIt** and **#ThinkItChallenge**, and I'll share your posts. I'm also active on Substack sharing weekly posts to help you create and live your dream life. Follow @sarahcentrella The Coaching Corner.

You've already done the hard part by finishing this book. Now let's turn what you know into the life you want.

You ready? Let's fucking go!

A Note from the Author

I always knew June 2025 was going to be a crazy month—one filled with some of life's biggest milestones for my little family. It's a month that I've been planning for on my #Futureboard, and written about in my Life Plan Story, for literally the past ten years.

I knew it would be a lot—but in a good way. All the changes ahead were major life moments, yes, but exciting ones. My twin daughters, Mira and Izzy, would be graduating high school and turning eighteen, marking the end of an era. Just two weeks later, my son Kanen would graduate from the University of Oregon and head off to start his new life in Texas, working for the College Football Playoffs. In the middle of it all, I'd be turning fifty—and after seventeen years of raising my three kids on my own, I'd officially become an empty nester. Add in my first international vacation with my man, meeting all his friends and family at his best friend's wedding, and it was shaping up to be an epic month.

It all kicked off on June 1st when I turned in the manuscript for this book to my publisher. I was so happy to have hit my deadline—the month was officially off to a roaring, celebratory start.

Everything was going to plan on June 16 as we settled into our seats at Kanen's graduation and the processional began. I'd successfully gotten through all the girls' celebrations and could now turn my attention to my son's big moment. I hugged my family and scanned the crowd of graduates, searching for my son. My brother Jeremiah was the first to spot him, and we all shared the joy of seeing Kanen—and of him spotting us in return.

When the song "Coming Home" started playing, the weight of the moment—and everything this month had brought—hit me all at once. It was the same song that always played during the second quarter of every home game over the four years Kanen played for the Ducks. A song we'd shared together so many times in that stadium. I started to cry, and Jeremiah, sitting next to me, wrapped his arm around me in a tight hug. I rested my head on his shoulder and let it all out. He knew exactly what that moment meant—for me, for Kanen, and for our whole family.

He told me how proud he was of me—of everything I'd accomplished and all the work, pain, and sacrifice it took to get to this moment. He said how proud he was of Kanen and my girls too. He said everything I'd ever needed to hear from my brother—the one who's always been the most successful, well-traveled, smartest, and most accomplished person I know. He's been the rock of our family and his community. His opinion and validation have always meant more to me than anyone else's. His success has been a constant push for me to chase my goals and keep going after my dreams.

Most girls grow up needing their father to be proud of them. I needed Jeremiah to be proud of me. His words in that moment meant everything, and I told him so.

I thanked him for inspiring Kanen to go to college and for always encouraging him to work hard in school. He used to reward Kanen for getting good grades and was the one who taught him to start investing when he was just sixteen—sparking his passion for finance and helping him break our family's generational cycle of financial struggle. My brother had broken that cycle for himself, and he was determined to pass on what he'd learned so my kids wouldn't have to face the same hardships I did. He has poured into them in so many ways. He's been the man in their lives, the only solid male role model they've ever had.

After graduation was over, we rushed out to grab a quick hug from Kanen before he had to head off to his Business School ceremony. We had just enough time for everyone to share a big meaningful hug, a few happy tears, and snap some quick photos. Then he was off with the other graduates, and it was time to say goodbye to the rest of my family as they headed back home to Portland. I paused to give Jeremiah an extra tight hug and thanked him—for showing up that day and always.

That was Monday.

On Tuesday, I began preparing for my 50th birthday party, which would be the following day. It was the first birthday party I'd ever planned for myself in my entire life. It was going to be a fun relaxed dinner prepared by Jeremiah, who is an exceptional gourmet chef and the owner of the gourmet food company *Wolfella*. He and I had finalized the menu on Monday at graduation, and I was excited for all my friends to taste his cooking.

I woke up Wednesday morning, June 18, 2025 filled with excitement and a long to-do list. I ran all the last-minute errands a party requires—got my nails and lashes done, finalized my outfit, and packed my suitcase. I couldn't decide what I was more excited about: the dinner party that night or leaving it at 9:30 to race to the airport with my love and catch a flight to Mexico to celebrate.

It was a lot—but all so exciting and monumental, I tried hard to cherish the moments and be present, knowing they'd all be gone before I knew it. My heart was full of anticipation as my daughters and I arranged the flowers for the party, and I quickly texted Jeremiah to confirm the address and what time he planned to arrive.

I was curling my hair when my phone rang.

It was my sister, so I figured she'd be asking what to bring or wanting to know what to wear. I answered it cheerily.

And then the world stopped moving. The curling iron dropped into the sink.

She was hysterical—could not breathe, could not get a word out.

"What's wrong?" I begged her to tell me, but she couldn't.

Years seemed to pass before she was finally able to say it.

"Jeremiah is dead."

My mind could not comprehend anything she was trying to tell me. It was impossible. I'd just texted him to confirm that I'd be bringing serving dishes. How could he be dead?

And *what does dead even mean?* My mind screamed.

That he's not feeling well? That he can't come to the party tonight? That he's at the hospital?

What does she mean?

Because my brother—the one I'd seen two days before—was absolutely not dead. He was cooking dinner for my party tonight. She must have it wrong. We had just seen him, and he was perfectly fine.

The shock and emotional whiplash of that day is impossible to describe. Asking my brain to get out of party-planning mode and into the reality that my brother—at forty-six years old—had just dropped dead in the kitchen while cooking, did not compute.

It was impossible.

Jeremiah Centrella was a loving husband to his wife, Margaret, and a devoted father to his two precious daughters, Lana and Eddy. He was the best brother to my sister Emielle and me, and the "fun, awesome, interesting, cool" uncle to Kanen, Mira, Izzy, Sam, and Lydia.

The NGO world knew him as a renowned corporate attorney, humanitarian, and advocate. He had an illustrious legal career including ten years at Mercy Corps where he served as General Counsel for several years. While there, he traveled extensively to Somalia, Afghanistan, Syria, Iraq, Tunisia, and Gaza (where he was briefly kidnapped by Hamas, released only when they realized they had the wrong person) and many more countries—negotiating with world leaders and sharing meals with locals.

His friends and family knew him as the larger-than-life free spirit who had a passion for seeing the world and floating a river. He once rode a yak across Mongolia, biked through Europe and North Africa at eighteen, regularly camped off the grid, and organized epic annual white-water rafting trips for friends and family.

He was a fearless skier, teaching his daughters and my son to ski as soon as they could walk. He could make a meal out of what he gathered in the forest—and just as easily prepare a Michelin-worthy dinner for friends on a private island or a backyard. He was the best and most passionate cook I've ever known and believed strongly, as I do, that a good meal with the ones you love can solve just about anything.

A dreamer who followed his heart, he left an extremely successful and lucrative law career to pursue his passion and launch *Wolfella* three years ago. He regularly advised world leaders, negotiated with corporate giants, and was sought after for expert commentary by outlets like *The New York Times*.

His accomplishments are even more impressive when you learn his origin story. Like me, Jeremiah was raised in poverty, off the grid in the Oregon coastal forest, and was "homeschooled" (though our mother didn't actually school us) until the fourth grade. He went on to attend a tiny rural high school, where he graduated at the top of his class and earned a full-ride academic scholarship to Colorado College and a law degree from Willamette University School of Law.

He defied the odds and never let his upbringing hold him back from pursuing his outlandish dreams. Instead, he channeled that early hardship and adversity into empathy and curiosity about the world around him. It fueled his passion for making a difference and creating a lasting legacy. His life made a real impact on this world, and for that I'm so proud of him. I'll continue striving to do the same, in his honor.

He was the kind of uncle who brought yak boots back from Mongolia for (then baby) Kanen, even though he was traveling with nothing but a backpack. The kind who took my son to get his first suit and had it tailored when Kanen went off to college. Who hired my daughters to work alongside him in his *Wolfella* kitchen during their high school summer breaks. The kind who brought back unused currency from every country he visited to gift to my kids every Christmas—regaling them with stories from each place.

He always showed up. He came to the games, celebrated the big wins, and gave the best hugs when you needed one most. He was the best brother, unequivocally there for me and the people he loved. His joy and pride when I became a published author was the best feeling, especially considering the childhood we both overcame to accomplish our dreams.

He truly was one of a kind.

I will miss you forever little brother.

Jeremiah died of a sudden heart attack with no warning signs or pre-symptoms on June 18; he was forty-six years young.

Life is a gift. Hug the ones you love. Tell them you are proud of them. Live life unafraid. Love this world and the people in it, take care of each other.

And…float easy.

Acknowledgments

I want to thank my amazing literary agent, Beth Davey, who believed in me long before I was a writer worth believing in. For over a decade, she's championed my voice, my mission, and my passion—and has repeatedly made the impossible possible.

Thank you to Anthony, who pushed me to get back into writing at a time when I was questioning whether I should keep going. He encouraged me to write this book, gave me the idea to add graphics, and even found Substack for me, which has reignited my passion for writing. Your insights, never ending support, and encouragement have been invaluable. I am forever grateful, Amore Mio.

Thank you to my clients over the past eleven years who've helped me learn how to teach these methods in a way that resonates and gets results.

Thank you to my aunt Maria Centrella, who was my first editor back when I was learning how to read and write at around age twelve (it's a whole thing—read my childhood memoir *Anomaly* on my Substack). She'd proof my short stories with red ink, usually crossing out nearly every word, and send them back for a rewrite. Every time I sent a corrected version—after looking up all the words in the dictionary—she'd send me ten dollars. And to this day, she's still the first person I send my manuscripts to for honest, objective feedback. Love you, Auntie!

Thanks to my ride-or-die girlfriends who've always got my back, Courtney and Jackie, love you!

And a huge thank you to my three beautiful children. Kanen, Mira, and Izzy, you always believed in me through the highs and lows of this journey. I am so insanely proud of the incredible young people you've all become; everything I do, I do for you. Mama loves you. PS, thanks Izzy for the help proofing this book!

And last, but absolutely not least—thank you, dear reader. You are the reason I wrote this book. Thank you for getting it, for doing the "Personal Work" sections as you went, and for sharing these tools and this book with someone you love. In doing that, you're passing along knowledge that someone else needs. Let's create a movement. Together, we can change the world—because mental fitness is the new self-care.